# From Epiphany to Lent

# From Epiphany to Lent

## Daily Readings and Meditations to Pray Alone or as a Family

Fr. Patrick Troadec, SSPX

Translated by Ann Marie Temple

**Angelus Press**

PO Box 217 | Saint Marys, KS 66536

Original edition, *De l'Epiphanie au Carême, au jour le jour,* published by Via Romana, 2015

Translated from the French by Ann Marie Temple.

Cover: *The Wedding Feast at Cana*, 1819 (oil on canvas), Julius Schnorr von Carolsfeld (1794-1872). Hamburger Kunsthalle, Hamburg, Germany / Bridgeman Images.

Library of Congress Control Number: 2019957031

© 2020 Angelus Press
All rights reserved.

## ANGELUS PRESS
PO Box 217
Saint Marys, Kansas 66536
Phone (816) 753-3150
Fax (816) 753-3557
Order Line (800) 966-7337
**www.angeluspress.org**

ISBN: 978-1-949124-24-8
FIRST PRINTING—January 2020
SECOND PRINTING—February 2021

Printed in the United States of America

# Table of Contents

A Note to Our Readers _____ 1

**THE TIME AFTER EPIPHANY** _____ 5

**First Sunday after Epiphany** _____ 4
Monday of the First Week after Epiphany _____ 7
Tuesday of the First Week after Epiphany _____ 10
Wednesday of the First Week after Epiphany _____ 13
Thursday of the First Week after Epiphany _____ 16
Friday of the First Week after Epiphany _____ 19
Saturday of the First Week after Epiphany _____ 22

**Second Sunday after Epiphany** _____ 25
Monday of the Second Week after Epiphany _____ 28
Tuesday of the Second Week after Epiphany _____ 31
Wednesday of the Second Week after Epiphany _____ 34
Thursday of the Second Week after Epiphany _____ 37
Friday of the Second Week after Epiphany _____ 40
Saturday of the Second Week after Epiphany _____ 43

**Third Sunday after Epiphany** _____ 46
Monday of the Third Week after Epiphany _____ 48
Tuesday of the Third Week after Epiphany _____ 51
Wednesday of the Third Week after Epiphany _____ 54
Thursday of the Third Week after Epiphany _____ 57
Friday of the Third Week after Epiphany _____ 60
Saturday of the Third Week after Epiphany _____ 63

**Fourth Sunday after Epiphany** _____ 66
Monday of the Fourth Week after Epiphany _____ 69
Tuesday of the Fourth Week after Epiphany _____ 72
Wednesday of the Fourth Week after Epiphany _____ 75
Thursday of the Fourth Week after Epiphany _____ 78
Friday of the Fourth Week after Epiphany _____ 81
Saturday of the Fourth Week after Epiphany _____ 84

**Fifth Sunday after Epiphany** — 87
Monday of the Fifth Week after Epiphany — 90
Tuesday of the Fifth Week after Epiphany — 93
Wednesday of the Fifth Week after Epiphany — 96
Thursday of the Fifth Week after Epiphany — 99
Friday of the Fifth Week after Epiphany — 102
Saturday of the Fifth Week after Epiphany — 105

**Sixth Sunday after Epiphany** — **108**
Monday of the Sixth Week after Epiphany — 111
Tuesday of the Sixth Week after Epiphany — 114
Wednesday of the Sixth Week after Epiphany — 117
Thursday of the Sixth Week after Epiphany — 120
Friday of the Sixth Week after Epiphany — 123
Saturday of the Sixth Week after Epiphany — 126

# SEPTUAGESIMA — 129

**Septuagesima Sunday** — **131**
Monday of Septuagesima — 134
Tuesday of Septuagesima — 137
Wednesday of Septuagesima — 139
Thursday of Septuagesima — 142
Friday of Septuagesima — 145
Saturday of Septuagesima — 148

**Sexagesima Sunday** — **151**
Monday of Sexagesima — 154
Tuesday of Sexagesima — 157
Wednesday of Sexagesima — 160
Thursday of Sexagesima — 163
Friday of Sexagesima — 166
Saturday of Sexagesima — 169

**Sunday of Quinquagesima** — **172**
Monday of Quinquagesima — 175
Tuesday of Quinquagesima — 178

**February 2nd** — **180**

# PRAYERS — 183

Spiritual Communion — 184
The Mysteries of the Rosary — 185
    Joyful Mysteries — 185
    Sorrowful Mysteries — 185
    Glorious Mysteries — 186

# Table of Contents

Act of Faith _____ 187
Act of Hope _____ 187
Act of Charity _____ 187
Act of Contrition _____ 187
Prayer of the Angel at Fatima _____ 188
Prayer to the Holy Ghost _____ 189
*Memorare* of St. Bernard (1090-1153) _____ 190
Prayer to St. Michael the Archangel _____ 191
Prayer to St. Joseph, Patron of the Universal Church _____ 192
Prayer of St. Pius X to the Glorious St. Joseph _____ 193
Act of Confidence in God (St. Claude de la Colombière) _____ 194
Prayer to the Curé of Ars for Vocations _____ 196
A Prayer for Priests _____ 197
Litany of Humility _____ 198
Litany of the Precious Blood _____ 199

**Latin Hymns** _____ **201**
   Hymn of Vespers of the Holy Family _____ 201
   *Dies Iræ* _____ 202
   *Magnificat* _____ 204
Latin Prayer *Anima Christi* _____ 206
English Prayer *Soul of Christ* _____ 206
Hymn *Soul of My Savior* _____ 207

**Bibliography** _____ 209

# A Note to Our Readers

Dear Readers,

After the publication of booklets for Advent, Lent, and the Easter seasons, we now offer you one for the season after Epiphany and for Septuagesima. Its format is identical. Each day begins with a quote from Holy Scripture, generally taken from the liturgical text of the day or of the previous Sunday. There follows a meditation inspired by the writings of St. John Chrysostom, Bossuet, and Bourdaloue, as well as other more recent authors noted for their piety.

Two thoughts, most often taken from saints' writings, help to deepen this meditation. We then propose two prayers and a few concrete resolutions so that the meditation might bear abundant fruit and have lasting effects. The exercise does not exceed two pages per day.

Finally, to nourish piety, we include a few prayers and hymns at the back of the booklet in the spirit of the meditations.

This booklet unites two periods of the liturgical year. The time after Epiphany extends the season of Christmas and makes us better know and love Our Lord through the contemplation of certain scenes from His public life. The season of Septuagesima is a time for the deep reflections which prepare the soul for deep resolutions.

So as to keep in the liturgical spirit, the various themes considered in this booklet are all related to the time after Epiphany and the time of Septuagesima. Generally speaking, one theme stretches over the entire week. Thus, for example, the first week after Epiphany concerns the family; the third, the sacrament of penance; the week of Sexagesima sheds light on the parable of the sower.

This little volume of the Christian life may be of service to families by its simplicity and its practicality. Every member may draw some benefit for his own progress. In order to help this to be the case, parents may choose to simplify certain meditations to fit the maturity of their children. They may help the children to choose their efforts depending on their age, their temperament, and their personality. The prayers of the day could be recited as a family.

Everyone, whatever his state of life, will find matter for spiritual progress in this daily reading. Simply the thought for the day may sometimes be enough to inspire his meditation and give a beautiful orientation to his day.

Dear readers, I am very happy to offer you this new booklet and wish you a joyful time after Epiphany as well as a Septuagesima rich in graces, assuring you of my prayers and recommending myself to yours.

Fr. Patrick Troadec

# The Time after Epiphany

"The time after Epiphany consists of two to six weeks that call to mind the hidden life of Christ in Nazareth and manifest to us His divinity.

The time after Epiphany is the extension of the Christmas season. The divinity of Jesus continues to be in the forefront. Now it is Christ Himself who acts and speaks as God.

The Gospels of the second, third and fourth Sundays after Epiphany show us some of His miracles, and those of the fifth and sixth Sundays summarize His divine doctrine in a few parables. A man could not speak and act in this way if He were not God.

The purpose of this liturgical season is therefore to make us believe in the divinity of Jesus."

—Dom Gaspar Lefebvre

"The Sundays after Epiphany take us down from the mountain tops and we settle into the plains, amid green pastures, gathering what comes from the mouth of God, as the Communion antiphon says, with the sentiments expressed in the Introits.

The octave day [of Epiphany] marks the beginning of the public life of the Savior; the manifestation of the Trinity has taken place, prompted by the gesture of the Precursor. Our preacher from Advent comes back onto the scene. The Lamb of God is pointed out by name. He now advances toward 'His hour.'"

—Bishop Harscouët, *Liturgical Perspectives*, p. 107

# THE HOLY FAMILY

# First Sunday after Epiphany

## God speaks to us

*His father and mother were marveling at the things spoken concerning Him.*

—St. Luke 2:33

## Meditation

On this beautiful feast day, let us look at how the family can be a source of sanctification. It is indeed the setting most favorable to our sanctification, but for it really to be so we need to contemplate the example of the Holy Family, where each one fulfilled his mission so admirably. Let us reflect therefore on what God expects of us in the domain of the family. It is there that we can still truly make a difference, we who so ardently desire to restore a Catholic civilization.

If ever there was a happy family here below, it was the Holy Family! "In the home at Nazareth, there was never the least division, never the least dissension, never the least argument. The Holy Family was the perfect family, with all of its members in marvelous agreement because each was in his place and all were animated with the desire to please God and to submit their will to His."[1]

Jesus, Mary, and Joseph rendered to God all of their duties. They prayed together, they respected the name of God, His day and His Law. It was He who inspired their decisions and their actions.

How could such a memory not hold an irresistible attraction for spouses called in their turn to found a Catholic home?

The contemplation of this model allows us to realize what God expects of a Catholic couple. *Our Sire God being first served!*[2] It is before that

---

[1] *The Catholic Family*, Clovis, 2011, pp. 344-345.
[2] This was the cry of St. Joan of Arc; see Régine Pernoud, *Joan of Arc: By Herself and Her Witnesses*, Scarborough House, 1994, p. 195.

model that each member of a Catholic family must come to draw the strength he needs to fulfill all of his duties. It is there that each member becomes aware of his responsibilities and may then undertake his task with courage and perseverance.

Happy the families where the father hands down to his children the solid principles of life, and where the mother fosters in their souls a goodness that unfolds beneath the gentle sunshine of her gaze, so pure, so loving, so self-forgetful!

Happy the families where the man is the *lord*, and the woman is the *angel*! What a constant ascension of virtue, of esteem, of nobility do we see in these blessed homes!

O my Jesus, help me to understand the exact place that Thou wantest me to occupy in my family, and help me to fulfill it well.

## Prayer

Make us, O Lord Jesus, whom Thou dost refresh with heavenly sacraments, ever follow the example of Thy Holy Family.

—Postcommunion

*Or:*

Jesus, Mary, Joseph, give to my home and to all those who dwell there the peace and happiness of Nazareth.

—St. Alphonsus Liguori, HDD, p. 22

## Thoughts

- In the Holy Family, how well ordered everything is, how harmonious, how peaceful! The only rule is to serve Jesus; the only good is Jesus; the only love is Jesus.

  —Fr. Emmanuel, M, p. 36

- Look at a home where everyone lives only for God: is it not a little paradise?

  —Curé of Ars, R, p. 19

## Resolutions

1. To offer our communion for family unity.
2. To read the vespers hymn of the Holy Family.[3]
3. To set our screens aside (cell phone, computer, TV) and spend time as a family.

---

[3] See the text in Latin and English at the end of the booklet.

AN EXAMPLE TO IMITATE

# Monday of the First Week after Epiphany

### God speaks to us

*What God has joined together, let no man put asunder.*
—St. Matthew 19:6

### Meditation

God knows very well that we need concrete examples in order to make progress in life, and so He willed to give us all an ultimate model, both admirable and, in large part, imitable.

The example of Jesus Christ shows how highly God prizes the family. The Word, the Son of God, coming into this world to restore the human race, could have appeared all at once a full grown man, like Adam. Yet He chose to live and grow up in a home, sharing and sanctifying the conditions of our own life. For 30 years, He bowed to the unfolding requirements of childhood, adolescence, and young adulthood, before the mere three years of His preaching.

What could be the meaning of Jesus' dwelling so long within a family? It was not because He needed to do so. It is He who gave to the home of Mary and Joseph all of its qualities. As God, He had nothing to receive from them. But He willed to remain in that home precisely in order to show the importance of the family, for the family is where the children are born, and where they are prepared for the mission which they will one day have to fulfill in the world, just as Jesus willed to prepare Himself for His mission in the bosom of His family. What a magnificent lesson!

The example of the Holy Family teaches us first of all to carry our cross with love. The life of the Holy Family was not all roses every day. Let us think back on the particularly trying circumstances of Jesus' birth. Having to go from door to door in search of a welcoming house and seeing themselves rejected at every turn, having to take refuge at last in a stable for the coming into the world of the baby Jesus—what a heart-break for Mary and Joseph!

We can also think about the flight into Egypt. When the angel woke St. Joseph up in the middle of the night to tell him to take the Child and His Mother and to flee into Egypt—what an ordeal! To leave in the dead of night, toward a foreign country, without knowing where they were to live nor for how long—what a daunting prospect! What a source of anguish! But St. Joseph did not argue with the orders of the angel, any more than Our Lady argued with the orders of St. Joseph.

O my Jesus, that I might merit Heaven, help me to constantly do the will of God, and thereby carry out my own role in the divine plan.

## Prayer

Good Master, You willed to become a worker, and Thy divine hands knew the weariness of manual labor. Make a few rays of that hearth-fire of purity and love glowing in the workshop of Nazareth shine into those of our dear country, so that a rekindled faith might once again ennoble the poverty of my brothers and soothe their weariness!
—Pauline Jaricot, TD, January 5

*Or:*

Ah! May the Holy Family be truly the model of our own!
—Fr. Emmanuel, M, p. 36

## Thoughts

- How poor she is, the gentle Virgin Mary; how hard he works, the humble carpenter; how He suffers, how He obeys, the Child come down from Heaven.
—St. Alphonsus Liguori, HDD, p. 22
- Put on a heart of mercy, kindness, humility, meekness, patience.
—St. Paul to the Colossians 3:12

## Monday of the First Week after Epiphany

## Resolutions

1. To recite the fifth joyful mystery (see the end of the booklet).
2. To practice patience toward every member of the family.
3. To accept with an equal humor whatever the day brings, both the good and the bad.

## THE LORD OF THE FAMILY

# Tuesday of the First Week after Epiphany

### God speaks to us

*An angel of the Lord appeared in a dream to Joseph, saying, "Arise, and take the child and His mother, and flee into Egypt."*
—St. Matthew 2:13

### Meditation

The crisis of today's society is above all a crisis of authority. Teachers are mocked and policemen are attacked. These are signs that authority is despised.

The father is the first authority that the child encounters in his life. The man is the head; he is the rudder, the helmsman of the family. He chooses the direction to give the home. He has the grace of state to do so. That is why he does not choose that direction with a view to his own tranquility or his personal whims, but with a view to the good of the members of his home.

The head of the family looks to the common good of his family. He takes care that each member of his family be in his proper place. As a father, it is his special concern that the children grow, not only physically and intellectually, but also morally and spiritually. He needs to fulfill that role first and foremost by his own qualities, by his example, by his virtue. The head looks to the common good.

As head, he should not make his decisions all alone. It is he who must make the ultimate call for the major questions of the household, but before deciding he should discuss with his wife and take her advice into consideration. And he will always make every decision in view of the common good of the family and not in view of his petty personal comfort.

As father, the man communicates life. He transmits, conserves and develops the life of his children at every level. Certainly, he delegates to his wife a large part of the education of his children, but he remains the one primarily responsible before God. It would therefore be a mistake to say: the role of the man is to earn a living; the role of the woman is to take care of the children. The man needs to take an active part in the education of his children.

"Thus the father will avoid both extremes of imposing his viewpoint arbitrarily on the one hand, and abdicating before the most whimsical demands of his progeny on the other. He will also be conscious of the limits of his children and not demand of them more than they are able to give."[4]

## Prayer

Help us, O Joseph! Mirror of the most admirable paternity, be with us in our joys and in our sorrows, in our labors and in our rest.

—Pius XII

*Or:*

Glorious St. Joseph, obtain for me the grace to work with order, peace, moderation, and patience, without ever shrinking from weariness and difficulties.

—St. Pius X

## Thoughts

- Very early the father appears to the child as the head of the family, and this first authority leads him wordlessly to understand the authority of God.

  —Bishop de la Villerabel, PL, 1926

- The father teaches by example that life is not just made up of satisfaction, comfort and confidence, but that it is also made up of deprivation, loss, and fatigue.

  —Caudio Risé, AF, p. 9

---

[4] *The Catholic Family*, Clovis, 2011, p. 226.

## Resolutions

1. To pray to St. Joseph for our father, so that he might be faithful to his mission.[5]
2. To obey our parents as representatives of God (except in anything contrary to the Law of God).
3. To offer to lend a hand around the house.

---

[5] See end of booklet.

THE SUNSHINE OF THE HOME

# Wednesday of the First Week after Epiphany

## God speaks to us

*It is not good for man to be alone: let Us make him a help like unto himself.*
—Genesis 2:18

## Meditation

If the man is the head of the family, the woman is the heart; and as the heart, she has a complementary role to play: that of creating the unity of her home through affection. By her subtle psychology, she collaborates with her heart in the work of her husband and in so doing fulfills the plan which God conceived when He decided upon her creation. The divine Master willed to establish her as a help, as a support for her husband. She therefore needs to walk in the same direction as he.

Thus it is that God foresaw the role of the woman within the family and within society, and thus it is that she must conceive of it within her own generous heart, so full of devotion, so full of tenderness toward all that is small or weak, toward any that suffer around her, and above all toward her children, whose hearts she has a special gift for modeling in the image of God.

The reason for which our enemies have sought to take control of the education of our children from their tenderest age, is that they have understood the importance of those first years for the orientation of an entire life. It is therefore essential that mothers of families personally fulfill their role as educators, if at all possible, especially during the first years. "It belongs to man to shape the world, and it belongs to woman to form men."[6]

---

[6] *The Catholic Family*, Clovis, 2011, p. 34.

Consequently, the rebirth of Christian civilization will not happen without Catholic women. While it is true that the decadence in our society is due in great part to the promulgation of immoral laws, the reform of those laws will not be enough to reestablish order. To that reform must necessarily be joined the practice of the virtues, and in this domain the a key role falls to mothers of families.

Mothers of families, you are the salt of the earth, the sun of the family, and the family is the basic cell of society. You gave birth to your children in order to complete the number of the elect. It is not enough to have brought them into the world; you then have to lead them to Heaven. You will do so by giving them the example of your own virtues, in the footsteps of the Blessed Virgin Mary, and by fulfilling toward them your role as educator.

## Prayer

Come to our aid, O Mary, the most loving, the most faithful, and the most pure of all mothers.

—Pius XII

*Or:*

Raise me up to where you dwell, O divine Virgin, above the calculating ambitions of this world. Grant me not only to understand the greatness and the fecundity of sacrifice, but to draw its fruit and make its spirit my own.

—E. M. Lebeau, YW, p. 107

## Thoughts

- Remember that the child's first book is actually the heart of his mother; if this heart is all penetrated with Christian love, it will dictate to her the lessons proper to the child's understanding.
—Bishop Pasquet, PL, 1927

- That mother will never be equal to her task, who does not draw from the spirit of prayer and sacrifice the interior peace that she needs.
—Bishop Fauvel, PL, 1949

## Wednesday of the First Week after Epiphany

### Resolutions

1. To pray for our mother so that God might assist her in her mission, and not to forget this year to celebrate her birthday worthily.
2. To express today our gratitude toward our mother by a gesture that will touch her.
3. To recite a decade of the rosary for orphans and for mothers who are widows or alone.

# THE EDUCATION OF THE CHILDREN

# Thursday of the First Week after Epiphany

## God speaks to us

*Jesus advanced in wisdom and age and grace before God and men.*
—St. Luke 2:52

## Meditation

To educate one's children is to prepare them for their life as rational men; for their life as children of God, redeemed by Jesus Christ. What are these children, at the moment they come into existence? They are a mixture of good and bad.

The Church teaches us that original sin leaves something flawed at the heart of us, even after baptism. We call it the *fomes peccati*, the "kindling-source of sin," or else the "triple concupiscence." We also refer to it as the "old man." This evil consists in a type of blindness in our intellect, a weakness in our will, and a disorder in our sensibility.

Experience confirms this teaching of the Church. A child is not born good. Opposing forces wage war within him. Along with these inclinations common to all of us may come other defects tied to his genetic heritage.

Thus does the work of education consist in disciplining the tendencies of the child, in restraining his evil inclinations, so that his aspirations toward the good and toward virtue, placed in him by nature and by the grace of baptism, might come to full fruition. Those evil tendencies take over very quickly and so this training of his nature has to begin very young. As Fr. Caillon puts it, "a child of four has already gone through the printer."[7] So we can see the importance of those early years!

---

[7] Fr. Pierre Caillon, *A Child of Four Has Already Gone Through the Printer*, Notre-Dame de la Trinité, 1968.

## Thursday of the First Week after Epiphany

The reason education restrains those disordered tendencies is to allow full deployment to the forces of life. The whole being of the child begs for fulfillment. He looks to his parents for the energy and the orientation that will guide his faculties to their perfection through the practice of the virtues, and notably that of obedience. Education should be leading the child little by little to direct himself freely toward the good.

Let us raise our children in the love of God, in that faith which we received in order to pass it on to these souls which the good God has confided to us. Let us have clear principles in our minds and a firm will to apply them. At that price only shall we maintain joy and peace in our families, until the happiness of being all one day reunited in Heaven.

## Prayer

O Lord Jesus Christ, who, being subject to Mary and Joseph, didst sanctify home life with ineffable virtues: grant that, with the aid of both, we may be taught by the example of Thy Holy Family, and attain to eternal fellowship with them.
—Collect of the Mass of the Holy Family

*Or:*

May the unbreakable bonds of charity unite us, O God! May it foster peace in families and sweeten the bitterness of life!
—Hymn for Lauds of the Holy Family

## Thoughts

- There are not two educations, one to make the man and the other to make the Christian, but a single education for both.
—Bishop Louvard, PL, 1947
- Since the happiness of your children depends on your fidelity to the Christian Faith, their initiation to that holy Faith ought to be the principal object of your affection and your devotion.
—Bishop Rouard, PL, 1905

## Resolutions

1 To take special care with our morning prayers.

2 To read in the Bible the chapter on original sin (Gen. 3).

3 To make a concrete effort to practice the virtue which I lack the most.

PARENTAL AUTHORITY

# Friday of the First Week after Epiphany

## God speaks to us

*Jesus went down with them and came to Nazareth, and was subject to them.*

—St. Luke 2:51

## Meditation

To fulfill their task as educators, parents have received from God two admirable resources: authority and love.

Authority is the moral power to govern and to command. Parents have this power over their children. To them does it pertain to tell their children what they ought to do, to guide them, to obtain from them whatever their true good demands.

As Pope Pius XI said, "Parents therefore should be careful to make right use of the authority given them by God, whose vicars in a true sense they are. This authority is not given for their own advantage, but for the proper up-bringing of their children in a holy and filial 'fear of God, the beginning of wisdom' (Ps. 110:10), on which foundation alone all respect for authority can rest securely; and without which, order, tranquility and prosperity, whether in the family or in society will be impossible."[8]

Without authority in the parents, without respect in the children, education becomes a very difficult task indeed, not to say impossible.

Today, in order to restore both authority and respect, it is necessary that parents and children understand their basis.

When we say authority, we do not mean constraint. It is not a force in the hands of the parents meant to substitute for the weakness of the

---

[8] *Divini Illius Magistri: On the Christian Education of Youth*, December 31, 1939, Angelus Press, 2000, p.43.

child and render pointless any effort on his part. Authority is essentially educational. It teaches, rouses to effort, reproves, corrects, encourages; it incites to action. The goal of authority is not to obtain a certain outward order, but to help the children learn how to direct themselves and soon to act by themselves.

"Firm parents therefore express with confidence their wishes and their clear orders. It is they who determine the rules and they also who deliver the consequences. They also know how to exercise all patience and perseverance, whenever needful."[9]

Moreover, if their authority is to be credible, it is essential that parents maintain their own actions in harmony with their principles.

## Prayer

Jesus, Mary, Joseph, grant that our family life might bring forth that same charm of grace and virtue that flourished in your home.
—Hymn for Vespers of the Holy Family

*Or:*

O Jesus, obedient to Thy parents, glory be to Thee forever, as to the supreme Father and the Holy Ghost. Amen.
—Hymn for Vespers of the Holy Family

## Thoughts

- We have been fed on the idea that we have many rights and few duties. The opposite is true.
  —*The Friend of Parish Clergy*, XVIII, p. 495

- Authority should dominate without haughtiness; it should be paternal, but without weakness.
  —*The Friend of Parish Clergy*, XVIII, p. 496

---

[9] *The Catholic Family*, Clovis, 2011, p. 217.

## Friday of the First Week after Epiphany

## Resolutions

1. To make an examination of conscience as to our way of commanding and our way of obeying.
2. To recite a prayer to St. Joseph for civil and religious authorities.[10]
3. To enlighten and encourage a child or an adolescent in difficulty.

---

[10] See end of booklet.

PARENTAL LOVE

# Saturday of the First Week after Epiphany

## God speaks to us

*A new commandment I give you: that as I have loved you, you also love one another.*

—St. John 13:34

## Meditation

True education is a communication of soul. If it is not inspired by affection, it will fail. The child needs to find that he is understood. The family is that hearth-fire of love where the faculties of the child unfold in an atmosphere of confidence and security, thanks to the constant devotion of both mother and father.

Knowing how to love your children takes more than just wanting to love them. In order to love them rightly, you have to lift your eyes to Heaven and look at the way God loves His creation. Indeed, since you are collaborators in the work of God, you have to love your children in the same manner that God loves His creatures.

Your love has to be attentive and perceptive. God created us one by one and He sees us just as we are, with our own personality and with our defects and frailties. That acuity of perception does not take away from His merciful love; on the contrary, it makes that love all the more preemptive, all the more efficacious. Because He knows our weakness, God steps into the details of our life, adapting His action to our individual needs, making Himself our own particular providence.

Parents stand in the place of Providence for their children. In order to be strong and reliable guides, they have to know their children for whom they are, with their character, their tendencies, their qualities, and also their faults.

God loves us with a powerful love. He knows how to send us frustrations and how to make us suffer in order to hold us within our duty. He does not stop at our complaints or our confusion because He has our end in view and He wills to conduct us to it. Firmness is a form of love—of that love which means giving something of our own life for those whom we love.

God's love for us is woven out of respect. God respects His own work in each one of us; He respects our freedom, our spontaneity, and whatever it is that makes us different from anyone else in the world. Each being realizes a particular idea of God. Parents have to be mindful of what this divine idea may be. Education is not an assembly-line production. It demands discernment and respect for the given tendencies of the child.

Raising a child does not mean stifling him or taking possession of him; it means helping a personality to emerge and come into its proper strength.

In that way your children will grow up fulfilling all the promises of their baptismal grace.

## Prayer

O Mary, model of mothers, teach mothers—teach me—to form the hearts of children.

—St. Alphonsus Liguori, HDD, p. 141

*Or:*

Holy Family of Nazareth, shed upon our family the virtues, the peace and the joys of a truly Christian home.

—St. Alphonsus Liguori, HDD, p. 35

## Thoughts

- Joseph and Mary cherish one another and pour forth their mutual love on Jesus, who in turn offers to both of them the tokens of His charity.

   —Hymn for Lauds of the Holy Family

- To ensure the moral renewal of our country, the rising generations are going to have to receive a more virile education... Let us teach the child to use his will—teach him to *will*!
  —Bishop Maisonobe, PL, 1941

## Resolutions

1. To recite the act of charity, given at the end of the booklet.
2. To offer spontaneously to lend a hand at home or at work, without expecting anything in return.
3. To make a sacrifice, some specific action, which is going to cost me, in order to strengthen my will to resist evil and to strive for the good.

# THE MIRACLE OF CANA

# Second Sunday after Epiphany

## God speaks to us

*This first of His signs Jesus worked at Cana of Galilee.*
—Gospel: St. John 2:11

## Meditation

The newlyweds of Cana are certainly relatives or friends of Jesus and His Mother. Middle Eastern hospitality being what it is, Jesus very easily has His five companions included in the invitation.[11] Weddings among the Jews sometimes went on for an entire week. When Our Lord arrives, the celebration is already well underway. The coming of the new guests and especially of Jesus, who was so close to the couple, certainly fills the hosts and all their guests with joy. But soon the wine begins to fail, so quickly that a slight wave of uneasiness enters the wedding hall. The Blessed Virgin, with her feminine intuition, quickly sees the reason for the anxiety in the air. And so, to spare the young couple and their guests from such an embarrassment, she goes up to Our Lord and simply says to Him, "They have no wine." (Jn. 2:3)

There are six urns, or *amphorae*, in the hall, of a kind still to be found in the Middle East and used for carrying water or for keeping a supply of it at home, depending on the size.

The urns which are in the wedding hall can hold two or three measures, or around 50 gallons each. Our Lord is not miserly with His gifts. When He works a miracle, He does not do anything by halves. He is going to transform 300 gallons of water into particularly exquisite wine.

---

[11] Andrew and his brother Peter, with Philip, James, and John.

So the servants obey. They fill the jars to the brim with water and then draw out a sample—finding now not water but a most delectable wine, far superior to what was being served before. The difference is so striking that the chief steward sees fit to make a comment to the host. Like Jesus and Mary, let us do our best to save those around us from embarrassment when they are going through difficulties and certainly not complicate their troubles even more.

O my Jesus, help me to be kind and to practice an attentive charity toward the people around me, so that I might one day be shown to my place at the heavenly banquet of eternal bliss.

## Prayer

Jesus, my God, grant that our next communion might unite all of us to Thee and each one of us to the other, in truth and in charity! Amen.
—Fr. Emmanuel, M, p. 55

*Or:*

O holy and divine charity, gentle outpouring of the love which is in God, come into us and make us love everything that God loves and desires us to love.
—Fr. Emmanuel, M, p. 56

## Thoughts

- We have a wine of which we are permitted to be drunk; a wine which warms our veins, but with a wholly spiritual ardor; which makes us sing, but canticles of divine love; which takes our memory away, but only of the world and its vanities; which excites us to a great joy, such as the world does not understand.
—Bossuet, OW, I, pp. 293-294

- Drink all that you can of the sacred wine of charity: it will free you from those unhealthy humors that deform your judgment.
—St. Francis de Sales, TD, October 5

## Second Sunday after Epiphany

# Resolutions

1  To make a fervent communion.
2  To give alms to a beggar or say three *Ave*'s for him.
3  Take the time to listen to and console a person who is suffering.

MARY MEDIATRIX

# Monday of the Second Week after Epiphany

### God speaks to us

*Woman, what is that to me and to thee? My hour is not yet come.*
—Gospel for Sunday: St. John 2:4

### Meditation

The only two times in St. John that Our Lady is mentioned are when we see her at Cana and then on Mount Calvary, where Our Lord will say to her, speaking of St. John, "Woman, behold thy son." On Golgotha as at Cana, Our Lord calls His Mother by the name of *woman*.

Another detail which ties these two scenes together is the word hour, *hora*. When St. John uses the word by itself, it always means the hour of Our Lord's Passion.

Thus, when Our Lady points out to Him discretely that the wine is failing at the feast, Our Lord replies that it would not be opportune for Him to intervene because the hour of His Passion has not yet sounded. Our Lady speaks to Him of one thing and Our Lord seems to answer her by speaking of something else.

In fact, Our Lady is asking Him for material drink, while Our Lord has in His thoughts the spiritual drink that is to flow from His body pierced upon the Cross; He is thinking of His precious blood. When the Blessed Virgin asks Him to accomplish the miracle of changing water into wine, Our Lord moves beyond the present circumstances to the level of supernatural realities.

From that day forward, Jesus sees in His Mother the new Eve, who will be at His side on Calvary to engender us to supernatural life, to the life of grace, to divine life.

Understood in this way, Our Lord's reply has only the outward appearance of a refusal. In reality, it is a filial, delicate, masterful way of binding the shedding of His blood to the intervention of the Blessed Virgin, honoring her with a kind of right over all the distribution of this drink of which she herself is the very pure source.

Thus, beyond the miracle which it describes, the story of Cana offers a glimpse into the depth and riches of Our Lord's words, which already foretell His sacrifice on the Cross and remind us of the preeminent role of the Blessed Virgin in the plan of salvation.

O Jesus, help me from this moment to unite my sufferings to Thine and grant me the grace to give to Thy Mother her rightful place in my life.

## Prayer

O Mary, be my refuge, assist me, protect me, grant me to suffer patiently in this life, that I may have hope at my death and be crowned in eternity.

—St. Bernadette, R, p. 48

*Or:*

O Mary, fill me with zeal that I might lead to Jesus the sinners in my family who keep far from Him.

—St. Alphonsus Liguori, HDD, p. 129

## Thoughts

- The most Blessed Virgin stands between her Son and us. The more sinful we are, the more tenderness and compassion she has for us. The child closest to his mother's heart is the one who has cost her the most tears.
    —Curé of Ars, TD2, May 12

- You should take refuge in a Mother's heart, the heart of the Virgin.
    —Elizabeth of the Trinity, L 134

## Resolutions

1. To recite a decade of the rosary as a family.
2. To offer our sufferings by uniting them to the sufferings of Jesus and Mary.
3. To make the Blessed Virgin known and loved by those around us and to distribute blessed medals when circumstances allow.

THE WINE OF DIVINE LOVE

# Tuesday of the Second Week after Epiphany

## God speaks to us

*Do not think that I have come to destroy the Law or the Prophets. I have not come to destroy, but to fulfill.*

—St. Matthew 5:17

## Meditation

The Law of the Old Testament is essentially a law of the letter, whereas the Law of the New Testament purifies our hearts and little by little makes us resemble Our Lord.

This new Law, which is above all an interior law, is a law of love.

The Law of the Old Testament, an exterior law, was rather a law of fear. He who acts only by fear performs the action that is commanded of him, but his heart is not there.

Consequently, this external constraint is only stale, insipid water compared with the interior motivation which is love. He who loves adheres with all his heart to the intentions of the one beloved. That is indeed what Our Lord desires. And that transformation is symbolized at Cana by the changing of water into wine.

We can illustrate this shift from the Old to the New Testament by simply comparing God's manifestation on Sinai to Our Lord's presence on the Mount of the Beatitudes. It was forbidden under pain of death to approach Mount Sinai. Our Lord, on the contrary, invites souls to draw closer to Him: "Come to Me, all you who labor and are burdened, and I will give you rest." (Mt. 11:28)

Where does this transformation come from? In dying for us on the Cross, Jesus paid for our sins and rendered man worthy of divine adoption. From that moment on, the law of fear becomes a law of love.

Jesus wants to win our heart and so He attracts us to Him by His mercy and by gently stooping to our level. "Learn from me, for I am meek and humble of heart." (Mt. 11:29)

May we understand today this language of love, symbolized by the wine of Cana.

Let us drink this precious wine offered by Our Lord. What Jesus gives to the spouses at Cana is not just any wine. It is superb; it is the best that man has ever tasted.

O Jesus, I, too, want to appreciate at its true value this exquisite wine of divine love, in order to partake of the heavenly banquet in the blessed eternity of Heaven.

## Prayer

I love You, O my God, and my only desire is to love Thee until the last breath of my life.

—Curé of Ars

*Or:*

O holy Child, who have come down from Heaven out of love for Thy bretheren, give me a charitable heart, that I might take willingly upon me the good offices of charity.

—St. Alphonsus Liguori, HDD, p. 34

## Thoughts

- Jesus changes the Law into the Gospel, that is, the figure into truth, the letter into spirit, terror into love.
  —Bossuet, OW, I, pp. 284-285

- The water of the old Law becomes the wine of the new Law. This same water of the Mosaic Law takes a new form and a new vigor, when it is appropriated by Jesus Christ, true vine of the eternal Father.
  —Bossuet, OW, I, p. 289

## Tuesday of the Second Week after Epiphany

# Resolutions

1 To recite the act of charity (see end of booklet) with the firm resolution to love our neighbor as ourself.

2 To spend 10 minutes in the company of Jesus, always there with me, and to taste by faith the charm of His presence.

3 To manifest concretely our love for our neighbor by being gentle with him.

# THE TWO ENDS OF MARRIAGE

# Wednesday of the Second Week after Epiphany

## God speaks to us

*Increase and multiply, and fill the earth, and subdue it.*
—Genesis 1:28

## Meditation

Man and woman are complementary. Therefore, an attraction exists between the two, and we might imagine that the first end of marriage is to fill the void each one feels in solitude. It is not so. The Church affirms that the first end of marriage is not mutual support but the procreation and education of children.[12]

The primary mission of parents therefore consists in bringing into the world the children whom God wills to give to them and in educating those children in a Christian manner, so that they might one day contemplate Him for eternity. The mutual support of the spouses is the secondary end, secondary not in the sense of accessory or negligible but in the sense that the good of the children should pass before all else.

It is precisely for their children that the parents should try to live in harmony, because children need parents who are united, who are moving in the same direction. There is nothing more anti-pedagogical than division among educators. For children to grow up serenely, they need an atmosphere of peace and they need to hear the same kind of language from their father and from their mother.

Since this harmony between spouses is so capital, it is important to marry someone who shares the same ideals as oneself, to make everything easier. There have to be common and complementary elements, particu-

---

[12] 1917 Code of Canon Law, Can. 1013, §1.

larly on the essential points, to balance the differences that exist between man and woman and to keep those differences from degenerating into conflict. Anything else is a recipe for disaster.

A person has to have a certain maturity to be able to make so grave a choice. It is always painful to see young people playing with love before they are old enough to marry. They are preparing very sorrowful disappointments for themselves and complicating their lives. Unfortunately, this behavior is not at all uncommon, even in very Catholic families. May these young people open their eyes in time and have the courage to act!

## Prayer

St. Joseph, father and protector of virgins, make it so that, preserved from all stain, pure in mind and heart, and chaste in body, I might constantly serve Jesus and Mary in perfect purity.

—Prayer to obtain purity

*Or:*

Holy Mary, Mother of God, preserve within me the heart of a child, pure and transparent as a mountain spring.

—Fr. de Grandmaison

## Thoughts

- Love was not given to man for a selfish and personal end, but so that the joys which it procures might be poured abundantly onto new lives, issued from that same love.
—Bishop Picaud, PL, 1939
- Individualism wants an easy life, but it is a poor schemer.
—Bishop Julien, PL, 1918

## Resolutions

1. To recite a *Memorare*[13] for those who are single, that they might find a spouse pleasing to God.
2. To avoid all dangerous relationships in order to preserve the beautiful virtue of purity.
3. To respect the laws of life within the bonds of marriage.

---

[13] See end of booklet.

MARRIAGE AND THE EUCHARIST

# Thursday of the Second Week after Epiphany

## God speaks to us

*This chalice is the new covenant in my blood, which shall be shed for you.*
—St. Luke 22:20

## Meditation

In changing water into wine during the wedding at Cana, Jesus foreshadows the changing of wine into His blood and consequently also the sacrifice of Calvary. It is full of meaning that this sign should take place at a marriage. Jesus Himself is thereby making a connection between the sacrament of marriage and the sacrament of the Eucharist.

At first glance, that could seem curious. The two rites have nothing to do with each other. Mass and marriage are two very distinct realities. Nonetheless, it is not by chance that the Church associates them.

The sacrifices of the Old Testament already foreshadowed the sacrifice *par excellence*, that of the Cross, which is now renewed on our altars at each Mass. Before the insufficiencies of those sacrifices of the Old Testament, God Himself decided to take our human nature and accepted to die for us on the Cross in order to redeem our sins.

The first Covenant, which took place in the time of Moses on Mount Sinai, foreshadowed a covenant between God and men that would be even more beautiful, even more profound, even more solid.

In establishing the first Covenant, God promised to bless man and bound him to follow the Ten Commandments; so also, as Jesus contracts the second Covenant, He gives to His apostles a new Commandment: "Love one another as I have loved you." (Jn. 15:12) This covenant of love is therefore tied to a commandment of love. So it is that God has always willed that His covenant include a mutual commitment and that it be sealed with a sacrifice. Thus the words covenant, commitment, and sacrifice are intimately connected.

A Christian wedding, at which the spouses receive a ring on their finger as sign of their mutual love, is also a commitment which implies in turn an element of sacrifice.

May all spouses attain a love for one another that is capable of sacrifice.

## Prayer

Look, O Lord, we beseech Thee, upon these spouses, Thy servants, and graciously assist Thine own institution of marriage, whereby Thou hast ordained the propagation of mankind, that they who are joined together by Thine authority may be preserved by Thy help.

—Prayer of the sacrament of Matrimony

*Or:*

We beseech Thee, almighty God, to accompany with Thy gracious favor the institution of Thy Providence, and keep in lasting peace the spouses whom Thou dost join in lawful union.

—Postcommunion of the Marriage Mass

## Thoughts

- We must come to that holy table with a spirit of gratitude, renewing our good resolutions to practice virtue, particularly charity and humility, which are the proper fruits of a communion well received.
  —St. Jane de Chantal, R, p. 25

- Make use of daily vexations to mortify yourself, accepting them with love and gentleness.
  —St. Francis de Sales, XXI, p. 168

## Thursday of the Second Week after Epiphany

## Resolutions

1. To recite the act of charity (see end of booklet), asking for patience in daily trials.
2. To read the Epistle of the Marriage Mass.
3. To offer a little gift or a sign of consideration to a member of our family and to say a prayer for his intention.

LOVE AND SACRIFICE

# Friday of the Second Week after Epiphany

### God speaks to us

*Love one another as I have loved you.*

—St. John 15:12

### Meditation

In order to meet the trials of life with serenity, married couples experience the need to nourish their love at the Holy Sacrifice of the Mass, in contact with the divine blood received in Holy Communion.

The frequent reception of the Holy Eucharist is what allows the spouses to stay faithful to each other. At that moment they have within themselves their magnificent model for imitation and, above all, they receive Him who is able to open their heart as wide as His own.

Sacrifice really is the condition of genuine love, and we can even say that the depth of the spouses' love is in proportion to their capacity for self-denial. The more a soul is capable of sacrificing its little wants, its idiosyncrasies, its whims, the more capable it is of loving. And the trials dealt out over our lives are there precisely to enlarge our capacity to love. Without reducing conjugal life to the single aspect of sacrifice, nonetheless it is good to meditate on it from time to time, for it is too often forgotten today.

Love is at the source of the union of the spouses. In the beginning, that human love very often translates more into passionate-love or feelings-love than into gift-love. Yet, passionate-love and feelings-love are more about taking than giving. So there really is a true danger in reducing love to these forms, because man is not made first and foremost to take but to give, and to give himself. That is why, as passionate-love and sentimental-love lessen with the passing years, if there is no gift-love, if there is no gift of self, then love finally dies out—and thus in our day we have the sadness of seeing so many divorces.

On the contrary, those who feed their love at the fire of sacrifice know another form of love, which produces peace and joy in the depths of their soul and opens their heart to divine dimensions. As Holy Scripture says, "It is more blessed to give than to receive." (Acts 20:35) The sooner we understand that reality, the sooner we can correspond to the divine ideal.

May therefore the changing of water into wine at Cana help those who are bound in marriage to realize the role of sacrifice in their own life as well as the importance of frequent attendance at Mass for nourishing their conjugal love!

## Prayer

Accept, we beseech Thee, O Lord, the gifts of Thy divine Son which we offer to Thee, in order to draw down Thy blessing on the holy law of marriage.

—Secret of the Marriage Mass

*Or:*

Most holy Heart of Jesus, grant me an upright heart.

—St. Alphonsus Liguori, HDD, p. 163

## Thoughts

- To know how to love, is to know how to suffer.
  —Padre Pio, TD, October 24
- It is around the family hearth that one best learns self-denial.
  —Padre Pio, TD, September 16

## Resolutions

1. To make a sacramental or spiritual communion (see end of booklet).
2. To turn off our cell phone and stay away from the computer in order to spend a pleasant evening as a family.
3. To do something that costs an effort as a gesture to please another member of the family (*e.g.*, to clean up our things, to run the vacuum, to wait patiently before serving ourselves at the meal).

### THE POWERFUL INTERCESSION OF MARY

# Saturday of the Second Week after Epiphany

### God speaks to us

*His Mother said to the attendants, "Do whatever He tells you."*
—St. John 2:5

### Meditation

Epiphany means manifestation. What manifestation does it signify? It signifies the manifestation of the divinity of Our Lord.

Our Lord showed His divinity by inviting the magi kings to come and adore Him, but He also reveals it at Cana. That is why the Church brings the wedding feast of Cana into the mystery of Epiphany. This miracle really is an integral part of the Epiphany of Our Lord, because by it He manifests His divinity. But this mystery likewise contains the Epiphany of Our Lady, that is to say, it brings before our eyes the role of the Blessed Virgin in the history of salvation.

In the same way, if the feast of Epiphany is the feast of Christ the King, it also becomes the feast of the Queenship of Mary. By foreshadowing the elevation of Our Lady to spouse of the Lord of lords, of Christ the King, the episode of Cana foreshadows at the same time her elevation to queen.

How does Mary exercise her role as queen? In a word, by dispensing to souls all of the graces that they need for their salvation. It is at Cana that Our Lady first showed us the power of her intercession. Now that she is in Heaven, she still has the same credit with her Son, the same influence, the same power.

The Blessed Virgin's role as mediatrix in the acquisition of graces at the foot of the Cross earned her the role of mediatrix in the distribution of those same graces.

How then do we receive from Mary all of the graces that we long for? It is by recourse to her intercession, by prayer that we receive those graces.

At Pontmain, Our Lady encouraged the children to pray; she showed them the efficacy of prayer. "Yet pray, my children," did she tell them, "God will soon answer you. My Son lets Himself be moved."[14]

And it was just as the children of Pontmain were singing the *Salve Regina* that the inscription MY SON LETS HIMSELF BE MOVED appeared at the feet of Our Lady. Our Lord loves prayer made in honor of His Mother.

Let us realize today the importance, and even the necessity, of devotion to Our Lady.

## PRAYER

Blessed Virgin, obtain for me never to live in peace with the slightest sins.
—St. Alphonsus Liguori, HDD, p. 125

*Or:*

Hail, holy Queen, Mother of mercy, our life, our sweetness and our hope… Turn then, most gracious advocate, thine eyes of mercy towards us. And after this, our exile, show unto us the blessed fruit of thy womb, Jesus, O clement, O loving, O sweet Virgin Mary.
—*Salve Regina*

## THOUGHTS

- Hope all things from the powerful intercession of Mary!
  —Pauline Jaricot, TD, July 4

- Ask Mary, our Mother, to teach you to adore Jesus in profound recollection.
  —Elizabeth of the Trinity, L 136

---

[14] Apparition of January 17, 1871

## Resolutions

1. To recite a decade of the rosary for the conversion of a great sinner. Name him silently to yourself.
2. To have recourse to the Blessed Virgin in time of temptation.
3. To find the story of Our Lady of Pontmain and tell it to the children.

***Nota bene***: You will find the meditation for February 2 at the end of the booklet.

# THE CONFIDENT PRAYER OF THE LEPER

# Third Sunday after Epiphany

## God speaks to us

*Lord, if Thou wilt, Thou canst make me clean.*
—Gospel: St. Matthew 8:2

## Meditation

After the wedding at Cana, Jesus left Nazareth for good and settled in Capharnaum. Not long after, as He was coming home one evening, a leper comes up to him and begs to be cured. Just before, Our Lord had uttered the famous sermon on the Mount, which is like a summary of the new Law.

This sermon contains the eight beatitudes and invites the faithful to embrace evangelical perfection: "You therefore are to be perfect, even as your heavenly Father is perfect" (Mt. 5:48)—strong words, demanding words, startling and refreshing words, but at the same time discouraging words for those who know themselves to be sinners and believe themselves incapable of attaining such a height.

Whereas some of the people accompanying Jesus are probably giving in to grumbling or discouragement, a leper who did not dare to join the crowd of listeners throws himself at Jesus' and worships Him, crying out, *Lord, if Thou wilt, Thou canst make me clean.* Jesus takes the occasion to reveal the ineffable treasures of His merciful heart.

Let us turn our eyes upon the poor leper. Let us first admire his faith. Indeed, before asking for anything, the leper worships Our Lord and so reveals the spirit that animates him: a spirit of respect, of humility, of self-forgetfulness. Then, turning toward Jesus, he does not say, "Make me clean"; nor even, "Would You please make me clean?" He simply says, *If You will it, You can make me clean.* He believes, and rightly so, that for Our Lord to will and to do are one and the same thing.

Moreover, by leaving Jesus the freedom, in a way, to heal him or to leave him in his illness, he shows an admirable spirit of detachment. By saying, *If Thou wilt, Thou canst make me clean*, he is showing that he believes that health is not necessarily beneficial for everyone. *If Thou wilt*, that is to say, if You believe that it would be beneficial for me, then heal me. It is the explanation which St. John Chrysostom gives of this passage.[15] Such a prayer, full of faith, full of confidence and humility, goes straight to Jesus' heart, and He immediately heals this poor leper.

## Prayer

O divine Savior, I, too, am a poor leper; receive me: "If Thou wilt, Thou canst make me clean!"

—Fr. Gabriel, DI, I, p. 211

*Or:*

O Jesus Savior, I need Thee; heal me, have mercy on me!

—Fr. Gabriel, DI, V, p. 88

## Thoughts

- God never despises a contrite and humble heart. We have to ask Him for that spirit, so that our prayers go to His divine heart.
  —Pauline Jaricot, TD, September 22nd

- By the morning prayer, you open the windows of your soul to the Sun of justice; by the evening prayer, you close them to the darkness of Hell.
  —St. Francis de Sales, TD, May 16

## Resolutions

1. To recite the act of confidence in God[16] for the intention of the gravely ill, that they might have the courage to accept their trial.
2. To pray to the Holy Ghost[17] for the grace of final perseverance.
3. To visit a sick person when the opportunity arises.

---

[15] St. John Chrysostom, Sermon 25:2 on the Gospel of St. Matthew, in *Nicene and Post-Nicene Fathers*, First Series, Vol. 10, Christian Literature Publishing Co., 1888.
[16] See end of booklet.
[17] See end of booklet.

## THE HEALING OF THE LEPER

# Monday of the Third Week after Epiphany

### GOD SPEAKS TO US

*I will; be thou made clean.*
—Gospel of Sunday: St. Matthew 8:3

### MEDITATION

Jesus heals the leper because He wills it, and He does so using His humanity as a channel. Jesus calls upon His words, His hands and His will to work this healing. Obviously, He also calls upon His divine power, but that power is an incarnate power, a sensible, visible power, because it is present in a human body.

Yes, here on earth, grace is communicated to us through sensible realities. We receive grace through the sacraments, which are sensible signs, signs that we can see and touch and hear. For example, the water of baptism and the oil of the sick are sensible realities, as are the words that accompany these sacraments.

Grace is therefore communicated to us by Our Lord through His humanity.

In this particular miracle, we may be surprised that Jesus would touch the leper, since the Mosaic Law forbade doing so. To understand Jesus' action, we have to know that the purpose of this law was to prevent catching this contagious disease, and especially to prevent contracting a legal impurity. Leprosy is the symbol of the corruption of sin. Now, Jesus makes a point of touching the leper, "that He might signify by this also, that He is not subject to the law, but is set over it, and that to the clean, henceforth, nothing is unclean."[18]

---

[18] St. John Chrysostom, Sermon 25:2 on the Gospel of St. Matthew, in *Nicene and Post-Nicene Fathers, op. cit.*

And as we have seen, He touches the leper, He uses His body to accomplish this miracle, to show us that His humanity is the channel of divine graces. But it is God present in Him who works the miracles. Unlike the prophets of the Old Testament, who healed the sick in the name of God, Jesus now heals them in His own name. Whereas Moses prayed to God to heal his sister, who had caught leprosy, by saying to Him, "I beseech Thee, heal her" (Num. 12:13), Jesus merely says, *I will; be thou made clean.* He does not need to appeal to an outside power in order to heal. And His word is efficacious: scarcely is it spoken when the leprosy vanishes.

I, too, am sick, O my Jesus, and I beg You to heal me.

## Prayer

O God, who in creating human nature didst marvelously ennoble it, and hast still more marvelously renewed it: grant that...we may be made partakers of His Divinity who vouchsafed to become partaker of our humanity.

—Offertory of the Common of the Mass

*Or:*

O Jesus, life of my soul, make me rise again each day to a new life of charity and fervor.

—Fr. Gabriel, DI, V, p. 147

## Thoughts

- Daily in your prayers, with tears and sighs, confess your past sins to God.

  —Rule of St. Benedict, 4:57

- God will not be able to refuse you anything if you offer Him His Son and the merits of His holy death and Passion.

  —Curé of Ars, TD, April 14

## Resolutions

1. To recite the Fatima prayer several times during the day.[19]
2. To perform carefully our act of placing ourselves in the presence of God at the beginning of the various prayers of the day, that we might deserve to be heard.
3. To read the chapter of the catechism on the sacraments.

---

[19] See end of booklet.

THE LEPROSY OF SIN

# Tuesday of the Third Week after Epiphany

## God speaks to us

*If we say that we have no sin, we deceive ourselves, and the truth is not in us.*

—1st Epistle of St. John 1:8

## Meditation

In working the physical miracle of healing the leper, Our Lord had in view not only the salvation of the leper's body but also the salvation of his soul. He came to earth to save man from sin. And that man whose body was "full of leprosy" (Lk. 5:12), according to the detail in St. Luke, is the image of the human race, for, as St. Paul says, all men have sinned in Adam (Rom. 5:12).

Our Lord descending from the mountain and meeting the leper on His path is an image of the great mystery of His Incarnation. He left the mountain of Heaven to come to meet us in this valley of tears and to purify us of the leprosy of sin. Yes, leprosy is truly an image of sin. What leprosy does to the body, sin does to the soul.

To realize the tragedy of a soul in a state of mortal sin, we have to remember that we are on this earth to gain a treasure in Heaven. Our Lord told us so very clearly in these words: "Do not lay up for yourselves treasures on earth…but lay up for yourselves treasures in Heaven." (Mt. 6:19-20) Thus, every day, a soul united to God can acquire new merits, which increase the weight of glory that it will have in Heaven.

Yet, a soul which is separated from God by a grave sin can no longer store away anything for Heaven. It is condemned to sterility. Of course, that person may still perform good actions, he may still pray to God, offer help to others, make sacrifices. He may still do good, and even must do so, but not a single one of those actions can be meritorious for eternal life. Even if afterwards the person returns to the friendship of God, he cannot give back any value of eternity to the actions he performed while in a state of sin. That is a truth of the faith. All action which is not marked with the seal of sanctifying grace is therefore lost for Heaven.

But let that soul come out of sin, let it return to the state of grace, the state of friendship with God, and then all of its actions, however small they be, will be able to take on a value of eternity.

Lord Jesus, give me such a hatred of sin that I come to prefer death rather than commit a single mortal sin.

## Prayer

O Jesus crucified, grant me to understand the great wickedness of sin.
—Fr. Gabriel, DI, II, p. 89

*Or:*

Lord Jesus, who have so loved us, and who have so wept for our sins, grant us the grace to weep for them with Thee.
—Fr. Emmanuel, M, p. 104

## Thoughts

- We are all sick; the holy Church is a hospital where there is a great multitude of people with all sorts of sicknesses and Our Savior is our doctor.
—St. Francis de Sales, TD, February 24

- Even if you have caused Him pain, remember that abyss calls to another abyss and that the abyss of your misery attracts the abyss of His mercy.
—Elizabeth of the Trinity, L 298

## Tuesday of the Third Week after Epiphany

## Resolutions

1 To recite an *Our Father* and a *Hail, Mary* for the conversion of a great sinner.

2 To regret our sins profoundly, especially those which have most offended God, in order to avoid ever committing them again.

3 To stay in the state of grace at all cost, joyfully.

## THE VISIT TO THE PRIEST

# Wednesday of the Third Week after Epiphany

### God speaks to us

*Go, show thyself to the priest.*
—Gospel of Sunday: St. Matthew 8:4

### Meditation

What does the leper do, once he has been cleansed?

Our Lord does not let him go home right away. He asks him first to show himself to the priest and to present the offering commanded by Moses, to serve as a witness to his healing. We see there Our Lord's concern that we obey the Law. Indeed, the Law prescribed that in case of healing, one should go to present oneself to the priest, whose job it was to verify the cure.

How can we heal ourselves of the leprosy that is sin?

Baptism has of course purified us in the blood of Our Lord and has reopened for us the gates of Heaven. But alas! we are still weak and we need another remedy to keep us from straying from our sublime vocation. We know that remedy: it is the sacrament of penance.

Thus, what Our Lord said to the leper, He says again today to all those who are tainted with the stain of sin—that is, to every one of us: *Go, show thyself to the priest.* He could very easily forgive our sins without passing by the priest, but He does not wish to.

The general law of Providence consists in using certain beings for the perfecting of others. It is already the case in Heaven, where the angels in superior hierarchies enlighten those of lower hierarchies. It is likewise the case on earth, as we see here.

We therefore have to respect this divine pedagogy, this plan of divine Providence in submitting ourselves to men to whom God has given the power to forgive sins. Our Lord said it clearly to the apostles and, through them, to priests: "Whose sins you shall forgive, they are forgiven them; and whose sins you shall retain, they are retained" (Jn. 20:23).

In going to show ourselves to the priest, we are exercising humility and we are uprooting a little bit more the pride which, in us, is at the root of all our sins. So it is that we detach ourselves gradually more from sin and carry on our climb toward Heaven.

## Prayer

O Mary, my Mother, obtain for me the courage to go to confession as often as the security of my salvation demands.
—St. Alphonsus Liguori, HDD, p. 171

*Or:*

O almighty eternal God, look upon the face of Thy Christ, and for love of Him who is the eternal High-priest, have pity on Thy priests… Stir up in them always the grace of their ordination. Keep them very close to Thee, lest the enemy prevail against them, so that they may never do anything in the slightest degree unworthy of their sublime vocation.
—Prayer for Priests

## Thoughts

- Open wide your heart to make all the sins come out of it in confession; for as they come out of it, the precious merit of the divine Passion enters into it to fill it with blessings.
—St. Francis de Sales, TD, February 20

- The more we have recourse to the sacraments of penance and the Eucharist, the more the yoke of the Lord is gentle and loveable. Purified by these sacraments, our soul rises toward God all by itself.
—Curé of Ars, TD2, February 13

## Resolutions

1. To recite a prayer for vocations.
2. To begin preparing our next confession, deciding on a no-later-than date and marking it on our planner.
3. To forbid ourselves all sterile criticism of priests.

## THE PURIFYING BLOOD

# Thursday of the Third Week after Epiphany

### God speaks to us

*Without the shedding of blood there is no forgiveness.*
—Epistle of St. Paul to the Hebrews 9:22

### Meditation

The leper, once he is healed, goes to show himself to the priest and then offers to God two turtledoves. One of the turtledoves is immolated while the other is let free after being dipped in the blood of the first.

The first turtledove is a figure of Our Lord who is going to give His life for us and shed His blood for the salvation of our souls. The second, however, which is released after being dipped in the blood of the first, is an image of the sinner purified in the blood of Our Lord. That is truly what happens in the sacrament of penance: the blood that Jesus Christ shed for us on the Cross is poured out upon our souls. When St. Catherine of Sienna went to go to confession, she would say, "I am going to the blood of Jesus."

To help us realize the value of the sacrament of penance, it is good for us to remember that, in this sacrament, it is the divine blood that is purifying our souls.

This consideration ought to stir up in us a variety of sentiments. First it fills our soul with gratitude toward Our Lord, who accepted to suffer and die for us.

It should also settle our souls in a state of confidence. We hope in divine forgiveness, not because we merited such a thing but because Our Lord merited forgiveness for us, through the blood He shed during the Passion. To doubt the forgiveness of our sins is to doubt the value of the precious blood of Jesus Christ.

And so, when we come out of the confession, may our soul be at peace and may we take flight once again like the turtledove that was set free, once it had been bathed in the blood of the one which was immolated.

Let us therefore understand, in the light of this Gospel, the plan of God for us, the desire that Jesus has for our holiness, and let us not give in to discouragement at the sight of our weaknesses. Let us consider that Our Lord is truly merciful and that His one desire is to heal us from sin, which is a repulsive illness, just like leprosy.

Lord Jesus, I thank you for having so often purified my soul in the sacrament of penance. I have confidence in Thee. Come to my rescue; heal me.

## Prayer

Most innocent child Jesus, grant to the sinner always to approach the sacrament of penance with such perfect dispositions that he may gather its fruits abundantly.

—St. Alphonsus Liguori, HDD, p. 65

*Or:*

O Jesus, You who have redeemed me by Thy blood, grant that this blood might bear in me all its fruit.

—Fr. Gabriel, DI, IV, p. 220

## Thoughts

- When you have made a good confession, you have chained up the devil.

  —Curé of Ars, TD2, September 29th

- Blush for your infidelities toward God, but trust Him and abandon yourself tranquilly to Him, like a little child in the arms of his mother.

  —Padre Pio, TD, June 7

## Resolutions

1. To recite the Litany of the Precious Blood.[20]
2. To meditate for ten minutes on the love of Jesus manifested in the blood that He shed for each one of us.
3. To struggle against scruples by multiplying acts of confidence in God.

---

[20] See end of booklet.

FIRM PURPOSE OF AMENDMENT

# Friday of the Third Week after Epiphany

## God speaks to us

*Go thy way, and from now on sin no more.*

—St. John 8:11

## Meditation

When the two turtledoves had been given to the priest, the former leper shaved his hair and cut off his beard.

We have to realize that leprosy clung especially to the beard, but this rite once again has a symbolic meaning. Indeed, still today, on the day when the young man enters the clerical state, the bishop cuts five locks of hair, thereby showing that the young cleric commits himself to detachment from sin and from the goods of this world. And so this action performed by the leper is the symbolic expression of detachment from sin, of which leprosy is the image.

As a result, we, too, when we have been to confession, ought to detach ourselves from sin in order that the action of grace might produce in us all of its effects.

For we must not imagine that Our Lord expects from the converted sinner nothing in return. Recovered friendship demands stronger affection and greater fidelity, but this applies to both parties, because friendship is always two-sided. So God manifests greater charity for the repentant sinner, but the sinner in turn must offer to God very special tokens of affection and inviolable fidelity. If instead of rendering love for love the sinner despises these new marks of affection by sullying once more the pact of alliance, he runs the serious risk of one day suffering the rigor of God's justice.

Thus, converted sinners, who have received from God such the proofs of predilection, have a particular duty of vigilance to avoid falling into a state worse than where they were before their conversion.

Unfortunately, people often lack foresight or courage to break with the near occasions of sin. I know that the company of a certain person leads me to backbiting and calumny, but am I doing all I can to avoid meeting him? I have an inordinate attachment to a certain person, who is a source of sin for me. Am I doing all I can to break my ties with him? I know that television and internet are dangerous for my soul. Am I doing what it takes to avoid those activities or else to set limits for myself?

## Prayer

My God, I have offended you; I regret it, "because Thou art infinite goodness," and because sin displeases You. May I rather die than sin again!

—St. Alphonsus Liguori, HDD, p. 190

*Or:*

Enflame me with Thy holy zeal, O Lord, so that I may no longer tolerate in myself the slightest thing displeasing to Thee.

—Fr. Gabriel, DI, II, p. 93

## Thoughts

- We have to call to mind our sins, acknowledge and confess them before God, in order to humble ourselves and make a firm resolution to correct our faults.

  —St. Vincent de Paul, TD2, February 20

- After our confession, we have to plant a thorn in our heart and never lose sight of our sins.

  —Curé of Ars, ST, p 75

## Resolutions

1. To recite the act of contrition,[21] making a concrete resolution of amendment.
2. To flee from what is for me a near occasion of sin.
3. To make a sacrifice in reparation for a sin which particularly offended God.

---

[21] See end of booklet.

FAITH: SOURCE OF HEALING

# Saturday of the Third Week after Epiphany

## God speaks to us

*Amen I say to you, I have not found such great faith in Israel.*
—Gospel of Sunday: St. Matthew 8:10

## Meditation

Last Sunday we saw Our Lord recompense the faith of the leper by restoring his health and that of the centurion by healing his servant. Let us meditate today on that supernatural virtue which, though not the queen of virtues, because the queen of the virtues is charity, is nonetheless the foundation, the basis, the root of all the Christian virtues.

Faith is a source of salvation but it can also be a source of reprobation, alas. It saves us because we have "been justified by faith" (Rom. 5:1), but it also condemns us if we do not live according to its principles. St. James affirms this very clearly: "Faith without works is dead." (Jas. 2:26)

"Faith saves us in two ways, both as the perfection of our good works and as the source of our good works."[22]

Faith saves us as the perfection of our good works. What does that mean? Certainly, we know that, to please God, we have to do good works, we have to be upright, we have to mortify ourselves, we have to practice mercy toward our neighbor—but all those things are without value if we do not have faith. It is St. Paul who says it: "without faith it is impossible to please God" (Heb. 10:6). And the Church teaches it after him.

Faith saves us therefore as the perfection of our good works for, without it, the most beautiful works, the most edifying, the most brilliant actions remain without supernatural merit before God. Faith also saves

---

[22] Bourdaloue, *Complete Works*.

us as the source of our good works, for it is from faith that comes the holy zeal which moves us to perform them.

How we ought to thank God for this gift of faith! How we must pray to Him, that He might grant to us always to preserve our faith inviolate! For, let us not forget, "he who believes and is baptized shall be saved, but he who does not believe shall be condemned" (Mk. 16:16).

I believe, O my Jesus, and I wish to prove it in my life by the works of faith, so as to reach the eternal happiness of Heaven.

## Prayer

My God, see the sincerity of my faith and the simplicity of my heart which seeks Thee; come and perfect these dispositions...

—Pauline Jaricot, TD, February 14

*Or:*

O my Savior and my God, grant us to see things with Thine eyes, as Thou seest them!

—St. Vincent de Paul, TD2, January 19

## Thoughts

- "We have come to know and to believed in the love that God has for us" (I Jn. 4:16) That is our great act of faith, the way to repay our God love for love.

    —Elizabeth of the Trinity, *Heaven in Faith* 20[23]

- The most subtle temptations are temptations against the faith. To overcome these, take care not to turn them over in your mind, but try to distract yourself and sweep those thoughts away the second they come, as you would sweep away a spark that had fallen on your clothing.

    —St. Alphonsus Liguori, HDD, p. 324

---

[23] In Elizabeth of the Trinity, *Complete Works*, vol. I: *I Have Found God*, ICS Publications, 1984, p. 180.

## Resolutions

1. To recite the act of faith.[24]
2. To look back over the events of the day in the light of faith and see Providence at work in our life.
3. To defend the Catholic Faith calmly and firmly when it is attacked. To look for the most convincing arguments.

---

[24] See end of booklet.

# THE CALMING OF THE STORM

# Fourth Sunday after Epiphany

## God speaks to us

*Peace, be still!*

—St. Mark 4:39

## Meditation

Our Lord lived at Capharnaum during His public life and He very often had to take a boat to reach the opposite side of Lake Tiberias.

One evening, as He is crossing the lake with His disciples, Jesus falls asleep in the little craft, and St. Luke even gives us the touching detail that He is resting on a pillow, showing us the simplicity of Our Lord.

But all of a sudden the wind rises and a violent storm sweeps over the lake. The boat is thrown this way and that and seems on the point of capsizing. The waves crash over the sides and threaten to drag everything down to the deep, boat and men together.

In the midst of this danger, there is Our Lord still sleeping profoundly: "but He was asleep." (Mt. 8:24) What do the apostles do? At first, full of respect for their divine Master, they do not dare to wake Him. They must certainly have been reassured by Jesus' presence, but it worries them that He is asleep. What if the boat were to tip over? In some climax of the storm the apostles yield to their fear and rush over to Our Lord.

In a panic they wake Him up, crying, "Lord, save us! We are perishing!" (Mt. 8:25). Very calm, very serene, fully master of Himself, Jesus begins by reproaching them for their unbelief: "Why are you fearful, O you of little faith?" (Mt. 8:26).

Even before working any miracle, Our Lord pacifies the souls of the apostles by reawakening their faith and their hope. Then, standing up, He commands the wind and the sea. Without doing anything complicated, without taking up a stick or raising His hand to Heaven as Moses had done, without even pausing for a moment to pray, by the mere effect of His will, Jesus calms the storm by simply giving it this order: *Peace, be still!* Let us admire here the almighty power of Our Lord. As a master commands his servant, as the Creator commands His creation, so He orders and the docile storm obeys.

Calm returns at that instant and the apostles find themselves on a lake now perfectly peaceful. We can imagine their relief. "There came a great calm" (Mt. 8:26), the contrast is striking. The apostles are dumbfounded. They are in admiration but seized also by a certain reverential fear before a miracle so dramatic.

Seeing such a miracle, O my Jesus, I, too, can only admire Thee and venerate Thee.

## Prayer

O Master of the world, may all creatures praise Thee!
—Fr. Gabriel, DI, I, p. 238

*Or:*

Take from me, Lord, all confidence in my own strength. Make me truly understand that I can do nothing without Thee.
—Fr. Gabriel, DI, I, p. 239

## Thoughts

- The apostles were only saved once they had recourse to Jesus; as long as they were exhausting themselves and struggling alone, they were having no effect.

  —Fr. Gabriel, DI, I, p. 237

- The Lord wants us to learn by experience that our effort is insufficient without divine help; that is why He leaves us in the storm until we have recourse to Him with total confidence.

  —Fr. Gabriel, DI, I, pp. 237-238

## Resolutions

1. To think back over certain moments in our life when God's protection was particularly evident, so as to strengthen our confidence in Him.
2. To be an instrument of peace, especially in our own family.
3. Quickly to have recourse to God in any temptation.

## JESUS, SOURCE OF PACIFICATION

# Monday of the Fourth Week after Epiphany

### God speaks to us

*Why are you fearful, O you of little faith?*
—Gospel for Sunday: St. Matthew 8:26

### Meditation

By His miracles, Jesus strengthens the faith of those whose good will has drawn them to Him. Thus, Epiphany is still going on, that is, the manifestation of God. Our Lord came to earth for our salvation. He is the Savior and He is the King. We see Him ordering the winds and the sea to be at peace and, at His mere voice, there falls a great calm.

The contrast is so dramatic between the storm and the serenity which follows that the apostles are seized with respect and fear. It is Jesus, the King, who commands, and already the Jews ask themselves, "Whence comes this transcendent authority?" *Christus vincit, Christus regnat, Christus imperat.* Christ conquers, Christ reigns, Christ commands. Since the time of Charlemagne, these acclamations of the reign of Jesus have echoed in our basilicas. The liturgy took hold of these cries of triumphant joy and raised them toward God. But in order for Christ to be the conqueror, we must put our own hand to the work. "Heaven helps those who help themselves," is the popular saying. We are right to proclaim the reign of Jesus, but we must do our part to banish and abolish whatever contradicts His reign in our life, in our families, and in society.

As we see Our Lord calming the storm, let us consider that God is a God of peace. Isaiah calls Jesus "the prince of peace." The Evangelist St. Matthew alludes to this prophecy in this verse: "Tell the daughter of Sion: Behold, thy king comes to thee, full of meekness" (Mt. 21:5). As St. Paul teaches the Colossians, the Savior, King of meekness and humility, has come "to reconcile to Himself all things" (Col. 1:20). In Jesus Christ, and through Him, peace has come to us. In His Sacred Heart, we find our peace and our reconciliation.

Now looking at our life, what keeps us in a state of agitation? Our unsatisfied desires? Our sufferings, which we have a hard time enduring? Our sins, which trouble and humiliate us? Anxiety about the future?

Acknowledging my misery, I turn toward Thee, my God, to discover Thy power, Thy goodness, Thy wisdom, Thy mercy. I beg Thee to console me, pacify me, strengthen me!

## Prayer

O Lord, I adore You hidden in the little boat of my soul. If Thou art with me, I will fear nothing.

—Fr. Gabriel, DI, I, p. 236

*Or:*

O Jesus, if the storm rises, I will take shelter in Thee, I will call upon Thee with all the strength of my heart and my faith, certain that Thou wilt give me that peace and that victory which I would seek in vain far from Thee.

—Fr. Gabriel, DI, I, p. 239

## Thoughts

- The interior storm of the apostles was their lack of faith. Our Lord wants to bring healing first to that interior evil; the rest will come after, if He so judges.

  —Fr. Emmanuel, M, p. 61

- If the aapostles had had enough faith, they would have been able not only to remain in peace, but even to sleep like Jesus, and with Jesus, right in the middle of the storm.

  —Fr. Emmanuel, M, p. 62

## Resolutions

1. To unite ourselves several times during the day to the Masses being celebrated throughout the world and ask that the blood of Jesus purify our souls.
2. To make short prayers full of confidence in God in times of temptation.
3. To reread and meditate on yesterday's Gospel.

# THE BARK OF THE CHURCH

# Tuesday of the Fourth Week after Epiphany

## God speaks to us

*Thou art Peter, and upon this rock I will build my Church, and the gates of Hell shall not prevail against it.*

—St. Matthew 16:18

## Meditation

There is a bark which has been navigating the changing waters of the human generations for the last 20 centuries. That bark is the Church.

Sometimes the wind rises in furious gusts, all the unbridled passions toss the frail skiff; consciences are in profound darkness and all we can see by the light of the lamps is the foaming crests of the waves ready to submerge the vessel. Thus, Pope St. Pius X said to the cardinals on May 27, 1914, "Alas! We are living in an age when men welcome and adopt with great ease certain ideas of reconciling the Faith with the modern spirit; ideas that lead much farther than one would imagine, not only to the weakening, but to the complete loss of faith. (…) Oh! How many navigators, how many pilots, and—God forbid—how many captains, confident in profane novelties and in the lying science of the time, rather than arriving at the port, have already capsized!"

Pope Paul VI himself was forced to recognize the existence of chaotic elements within the Church: "The Church finds Herself in a time of worry, self-criticism, we could even say auto-demolition."[25] Indeed, the situation has gotten so bad that a high-ranking prelate did not hesitate, 10 years ago, to describe the Church as a boat taking water from all sides.

What can we do in this situation?

---

[25] December 7, 1968.

First, let us learn to adore the mysterious designs of Providence. God permits evil always in view of a good, but in the time of trial that good is hidden. So we must not try to penetrate what is beyond our understanding, but know how to accept it.

We must also ask God for the grace of fidelity. In order to remain faithful, let us have at heart to know Catholic doctrine perfectly and put it into practice, let us be souls of prayer and let us take special care to remain humble, knowing that we are weak and that we, too, are capable of falling.

O Jesus, obtain for me the grace of fidelity to God and to the Church, one, holy, Catholic, and apostolic. It is that fidelity which will allow me to keep afloat in the present storm and come safely to harbor in the evening of my life.

## Prayer

Be blessed, Lord Jesus, for having taken us into Thy bark in order to lead us with Thee to Heaven.

—Fr. Emmanuel, M, p. 58

*Or:*

St. Joseph, patron of the universal Church, pray for us.

## Thoughts

- We must pray, pray very much, and beg Our Lord with insistence to remove the danger that threatens His Church. If the disciples had once called upon Him with confidence, even as He slept, they would not have had to struggle against the storm.
  —*The Friend of Parish Clergy*, XVI, p. 42
- When humanly all is lost, divinely all is saved.
  —Fr. Emmanuel, M, p. 58

## RESOLUTIONS

1. To recite the first glorious mystery for the pope, the bishops, and for priests.
2. To reread in our catechism the chapter on the Church.
3. To defend the Church courageously when she is attacked and to give the example of a holy life, in conformity with her authentic doctrine.

# THE SLEEP OF JESUS

# Wednesday of the Fourth Week after Epiphany

## God speaks to us

*But He was asleep.*

—Gospel of Sunday: St. Matthew 8:24

## Meditation

In this Gospel, there are two aspects to be considered. The first is that Our Lord is in the boat, the second is that He is sleeping. The fact that Jesus is in the boat should be enough to reassure the apostles, but the fact that He is sleeping leads them to panic. Let us recognize that we ourselves, unfortunately, often react as they did. *But He was asleep.* A strange sleep! A sleep willed for our instruction! Truly, Our Lord here means to teach the apostles the importance of vigilance, and to teach us, also, that we must avoid the sleep of the soul.

Certain of the faithful grow discouraged in sometimes enduring trials for which they do not see the cause and especially for which they do not see the solution. Many do not dare to blame God for their unhappiness, but they do not understand why He does not hear their prayers more quickly. And what is true for individual trials is even more true for trials that touch the Church and civil society. How many Catholics today would love to see a spectacular sign from God that reassures them and at the same gives time a good lesson to those who blaspheme His name!

Nonetheless, God does not abandon His children. Psalm 90, which we read in the breviary on Sundays at the office of compline, expresses the confidence which that man should feel who dwells under His protection. In this psalm, David shows that he who remains under the protection of God can overcome the most perilous dangers. At the end of the psalm, the Psalmist has God say, "I am with him in tribulation, I will deliver him, and I will glorify him" (Ps. 90:15).

Jesus is beside us in our trials; better yet, He is within us. He told us so Himself: "I am with you all days, even unto the consummation of the world" (Mt. 26:20). God is with us in tribulation, even if we do not feel it. Then, at the moment chosen by Him, if we are faithful, He will deliver us and at last glorify us in Heaven.

O my Jesus, help me to be untroubled at the sight of Thy sleep, to remain awake and confident among of the vicissitudes of the present life, in order to hold my sites on Heaven.

## Prayer

Sleep, stay asleep, Lord Jesus; but give us faith, and we will fear nothing.

—Fr. Emmanuel, M, p. 61

*Or:*

Lord Jesus, may my heart be for Thee a bed of rest. Long ago, Thou hadst no place to rest Thy head; behold my heart, Lord; enter in, take Thy rest, sleep. Sleep, Lord Jesus.

—Fr. Emmanuel, M, p. 60

## Thoughts

- The sleep of Jesus! A sleep of God in the midst of the turmoil of the world! The world is in agitation, it stirs up terrible tempests against the Church, and Jesus is asleep. He sleeps, yes, but His heart watches.

  —Fr. Emmanuel, M, pp. 60-61

- Fall asleep with a good thought. That will be an easy way for you to remember God when you wake up; and in the morning your mind will be better prepared.

  —St. Vincent de Paul, TD2, August 17

## Resolutions

1. To recite an act of confidence in God before the Sacred Heart.
2. To set a particular time by which you will go to bed, so as to get up earlier in the morning.
3. To pray with constancy and perseverance, without becoming discouraged when you are not heard.

LESSONS GIVEN TO THE APOSTLES

# Thursday of the Fourth Week after Epiphany

## God speaks to us

*The men marveled.*

—Gospel of Sunday: St. Matthew 8:27

## Meditation

Jesus could very well have prevented this storm. But He allowed it, and not without reason. The apostles had the privilege of being chosen to live near Jesus and announce the Gospel to the four corners of the world, and so there were two traps they had to avoid: the trap of pride in success and that of discouragement in adversity. To protect them against these two pitfalls, Our Lord allowed this mysterious tempest.

Up to this point, the apostles had been witness of miraculous cures, but those miracles were produced on others, whereas here, the panic, the fear for their life, is something they feel themselves. The contrast is so great between the state of turmoil and terror felt a moment before, and the state of peace and serenity which follows, that it marks the apostles for life. Let us note in passing the delicacy of Our Lord, who makes sure that there are only the apostles in this crew, so that the weakness which they manifested in that circumstance might be seen by no one but Himself.

Our Lord has just given the apostles an experiential lesson in their weakness and His strength, in their indigence and His power, in their misery and His goodness. They therefore understand that, in spite of their weakness, they have nothing to fear as long as they live near Jesus.

It is therefore in order to manifest Himself to the apostles and to stir up gratitude in them that Our Lord lets the storm break loose and then calms it, when He pleases.

Yes, this Gospel of the storm is certainly one of the most instructive for our spiritual life. It teaches us the need to keep watchful at all times. It shows us that, without divine assistance, there is not much to us and we can perish at any moment. It teaches us finally that trials are the lot of souls dear to God and that we should not be surprised at them nor anxious about them, for Our Lord will not let us perish if we have faith in Him.

O Jesus, it is with great confidence that I place myself under Thy protection in the midst of the storms of the present life, so that I might one day reach the harbor of eternal salvation.

## Prayer

Lord Jesus, increase our faith and we will not fear; increase our faith and we will sleep in peace alongside Thee.

—Fr. Emmanuel, M, p. 62

*Or:*

O God, who knowest us to be set in the midst of so great dangers, that by reason of the frailty of our nature, we cannot stand fast: grant us health of mind and body, that what we suffer for our sins, we may overcome by Thy help.

—Collect for Sunday Mass

## Thoughts

- Although you be launched out upon the waves and tossed by the winds of many vexations, look always toward Heaven and say to Our Lord, "O God, it is for You that I set sail and ride the seas; be my guide and my captain."

    —St. Francis de Sales, TD, January 26

- Let us have recourse to Mary, who is the sure haven of the shipwrecked, the hope of those who are without hope.

    —Pauline Jaricot, TD, May 20

## Resolutions

1 To recite a *Memorare* to beg the Blessed Virgin to help those who are discouraged.
2 To avoid building ourselves up in the eyes of others.
3 Not to be discouraged after we commit sins, but to regret them right away and make an act of reparation.

CONSOLATIONS IN TIME OF TRIAL

# Friday of the Fourth Week after Epiphany

## God speaks to us

*The world shall rejoice; and you shall be sorrowful, but your sorrow shall be turned into joy.*

—St. John 16:20

## Meditation

To help us to stay serene and not call everything into question when life becomes difficult, let us awaken the gaze of our faith.

What should reassure us first of all is to think that God is Providence. So even if there seems to be no justice here below, there will be on the other side. The Fathers of the Church constantly insisted on this fact against the heretics who believed in the existence of God but doubted the immortality of the soul. The Fathers said to them, "You believe that God exists. So, this God must love those who serve Him and strive to please Him. If He does not love them, where is His wisdom? Where is His goodness? If He does love them, when does He show it? Not on this earth, because very often He leaves them in affliction. Therefore, there must necessarily exist another life where He rewards them for their virtue."

St. Augustine reasoned in the same way when he said, "Look at things from the point of view of eternity and then you will understand why God seems to be so rigorous with His friends and so favorable to His enemies." The perspective of Heaven sweetened the trials of the just of the Old Testament and of the saints. It will also sweeten our own.

In the midst of our trials, we have another consolation, and these are the predictions of Our Lord. If Our Lord had told us, "The sign of predestination is earthly goods; it is the wealth and pleasures that I grant in abundance to those who love me," then we could anxious at seeing

God allow our lives to be riddled with trials. But the Gospel says nothing of the kind.

Quite the contrary, Jesus foretold even to the last details what the just would have to suffer, so that they would not be scandalized or taken by surprise. He even said, "These things I have spoken to you that you may not be scandalized" (Jn. 16:1) when the time for suffering has come, and that "you may remember that I told you" (Jn. 16:4). Let us not be astonished when trials fall upon us and let us console ourselves with the thought that Jesus ended His words by saying, *your sorrow shall be turned into joy*, "and your joy no one shall take from you" (Jn. 16:22).

## Prayer

O God, how I need to know Thine infinite love! To know in order to believe, believe in order to love, love in order to give myself entirely to Thee, holding back nothing, as Thou gavest Thyself to me.

—Fr. Gabriel, DI, I, p. 116

*Or:*

How your glances, O Mother of the Word, stir up hope in hearts crushed down by discouragement.

— Pauline Jaricot, TD, January 10

## Thoughts

- In the hours when you feel only oppression and lassitude, you will please Him even more if you faithfully *believe* that He is still working, that He is loving you just the same, and *even more*.
  — Elizabeth of the Trinity, *Let Yourself Be Loved*, 5[26]

- Death, life, illness, health, everything comes to us by order of Providence.

  —St. Vincent de Paul, TD1, January 21

---

[26] In Elizabeth of the Trinity, *Complete Works*, vol. I: *I Have Found God*, ICS Publications, 1984, p. 101.

## Resolutions

1. To recite the second glorious mystery, thinking about the happiness of Heaven.
2. To read chapter 6 of St. Matthew, on Providence.
3. To keep your smile, inwardly and outwardly, in the midst of adversity.

PATIENCE IN TRIALS

# Saturday of the Fourth Week after Epiphany

## God speaks to us

*In the world you will have affliction. But take courage, I have overcome the world.*

—St. John 16:33

## Meditation

When we become familiar with Holy Scripture, we are struck by the great variety of trials that the friends of God have endured, and especially the trial of time.

God, through the prophet Samuel, confers the royal unction on David; scarcely is he anointed when he must flee, persecuted by Saul, who wants to kill him. Where was the divine unction? Where was the promise for an immediate future? Right after his anointing, David finds himself in great tribulation, exiled to the desert, reduced to want of everything, even food, obliged to seek refuge among pagans, because of the traps that are spread for him. But David keeps confidence in the promises of God and at last, for his fidelity, God grants him to reign for many long years.

It had been so long since God promised a son to Abraham without sending him one and, in the meantime, how many trials did he not have to suffer! But Abraham patiently endures all of these difficulties and at last his wife Sarah, at 90 years old, brings a child into the world.

God gives the order to Noah to build an ark, when he is already in his 500th year. Having learned from God Himself that He would send a flood over all the earth, Noah carries out the work immediately. But the flood does not come. He has to wait 100 years to see the realization of what God had foretold to him. 100 years! And, marvelous to behold, not once over the course of that century did Noah wonder whether or not God would do what He had said; he keeps his confidence. That is why he would be saved at last, himself and all his family.

Let us therefore not despair when we see that God does not accomplish our dearest wishes right away, and let us believe in His almighty power and His merciful goodness, even if we do not see the effects immediately.

May this meditation offer us encouragement and support, not only in our personal trials but also in those that affect the Church and civil society.

I wish, O my Jesus, to remain more than ever attached to You by prayer and to brave with You every storm, in order to reach one day the harbor of salvation in the blessed eternity of Heaven.

## Prayer

Divine Heart of Jesus, I offer You, through the Immaculate Heart of Mary, the actions, the sufferings and the joys of this day, in reparation for my sins and for all the intentions for which Thou continually immolatest Thyself on the altar.

—Offering to the Sacred Heart

*Or:*

Lord, I want to do what Thou wilt because Thou willst it, in the way Thou willst it.

—Clement XI, Universal Prayer

## Thoughts

- Bear with the greatest patience one another's infirmities, whether of body or character.

  —Rule of St. Benedict, 72:5

- Why do we put up with one another? It is because in doing so we carry out the law of Jesus Christ: "Bear one another's burdens, and so you will fulfill the law of Christ" (Gal. 6:2).

  —St. Vincent de Paul, TD2, April 18

## Resolutions

1. To recite the fourth glorious mystery to ask Our Lady to sustain us in the last moments of our life.
2. To offer a sacrifice to obtain the conversion of a dying person.
3. To seek out and emphasize a quality in a person whose faults we find aggravating.

# THE GOOD SEED

# Fifth Sunday after Epiphany

### God speaks to us

*The kingdom of Heaven is like a man who sowed good seed in his field.*
—Gospel: St. Matthew 13:24

### Meditation

This man who sows the good seed is Jesus. With what care does the peasant prepare the seed that he intends for his field! He wants it to be of the finest quality. The chosen grain is passed through the sieve, sorted, any foreign elements or bad seed removed. Finally, before placing it in the earth, the peasant washes it again and puts it through a preparation which is meant to complete the purification and destroy any bad grain that could compromise its growth.

So does the divine sower act also. His field is the world. In this vast field, He has spread, and each day still spreads a most select seed, a pure seed without admixture: truth, grace, everything that can make man good and happy. O admirable and untiring sower! He sows everywhere and always, He spreads with abundance the most excellent gifts; He pours them into the reason, the heart and the senses of every soul of good will. He has sown His sublime teachings, His divine examples, His precious blood. He sows even now, and He will continue to sow until the end of ages by the hands of His apostles, of His Church, to whom He said, "Going therefore, teach ye all nations, baptizing them in the name of the Father, and of the Son, and of the Holy Ghost" (Mt. 28:19).

Such is the mission that the Church has received from her divine founder: to sow the good seed throughout the world, to take care that it grow, that it not be stifled by weeds, to bestow on it all the care necessary to help it to sprout and come to full maturity. She sows the good and can only sow the good. The men of the Church may, alas! be fallible, but the Church herself is infallible. Never can we detect the slightest error in her authentic teaching, nor the least defect, the smallest imperfection in her morals. Ah! if the action of God, if the action of the Church, His mystical spouse, met no obstacles, what a rich, what a resplendent harvest would rise up to eternity! From one end of the world to the other, we would see only nobility of soul, men loving God, devoted to their neighbor, united in the same Faith and in the practice of the same sublime and eminent virtues.

## Prayer

My God, guide me by Thy wisdom, hold me with Thy justice, comfort me with Thy mercy, protect me with Thy power.
—Clement XI, Universal Prayer

*Or:*

I offer Thee my thoughts, that they be fixed on Thee; my words, that they be of Thee; my actions, that they be according to Thee; and my sufferings, that they be endured for Thee.
—Clement XI, Universal Prayer

## Thoughts

- The course we have entered after baptism is like the fields at harvest. We have but to reach out our hand and gather up. After baptism, all the graces and gifts of Heaven are there for the taking…
—Curé of Ars, TD2, May 16

- Let us strive to perform our actions with the purity of intention of Our Lord in becoming incarnate and capable of suffering and dying: He did so with no other motive than the glory of His eternal Father and the salvation of men.
—St. Jane de Chantal, R, p. 10

## Fifth Sunday after Epiphany

## Resolutions

1 To recite slowly the act of charity, meditating on the words (see end of booklet).

2 To lend a hand spontaneously and to have the simplicity to ask our neighbor for help.

3 To read in our catechism the chapter on grace.

THE WEEDS

# Monday of the Fifth Week after Epiphany

### God speaks to us

*While men were asleep, his enemy came and sowed weeds among the wheat, and went away.*
—Gospel of Sunday: St. Matthew 13:25

### Meditation

Why is there so much evil on earth? What answer can we give to this grave question? Evil is a mystery, which we cannot fully elucidate. A mystery, by definition, is incomprehensible, inaccessible to our human mind. Nonetheless, through reason and especially through faith, we can shed some light upon it. The parable of the weeds and the good seed is going to help us to do so. After having spoken of the seed sown by the peasant, Our Lord says that, *while men were asleep, his enemy came and sowed weeds among the wheat, and went away.* This sentence shows us the origin of evil: *his enemy came…* The enemy of God is Satan, the demon, the devil. It is he who is at the origin of evil; it is not God.

And Our Lord does not merely teach us that the devil exists, but also He shows us his strategy, his tactic, his plan of attack. The devil does not come during the day; he comes at night. He does not come when people are awake, but when they are asleep. That is why, at the beginning of His Passion, at the moment when the hour of the power of darkness had come, Jesus said to His apostles, "Watch and pray, that you may not enter into temptation" (Mt. 26:41).

The devil sows weeds in souls. Why does he sow this particular weed, called "cockle"? Actually the cockle seed looks like a grain of wheat. It has the same appearance, it has the same outward aspect, it is simply a little bit darker.

The devil is wily. That is why he disguises himself as an angel of light. He does not present himself to us such as he is, saying to us, "I am the devil, I want to lead you to Hell, follow me." If he did that, no one would listen.

The devil is going to try to attract souls to himself by the illusion of virtue. He is going to camouflage evil by presenting it under an appearance of good, so that people will be tricked. By mixing error with a clever dose of truth, he brings down the weak and the naïve. And, unfortunately, we ourselves fall too often into his nets.

O Jesus, give me clearness of mind to discern the snares of the devil and strength to resist his seductions.

## Prayer

St. Michael the Archangel, defend us in battle. Be our protection against the wickedness and the snares of the devil.

—Prayer to St. Michael

*Or:*

Lord, forgive us our sins and may Thee Thyself direct our inconstant hearts.

—Secret for Sunday

## Thoughts

- The good grain is and will always be the only legitimate seed of the field of God, and it is the duty, it is the right of all men—fathers of families, princes, pontiffs—to forbid access to this field to sowers of weeds.

  —*The Friend of Parish Clergy*, XI, p. 38

- The weeds are especially impurity and pride.

  —Curé of Ars, R, p. 152

## Resolutions

1. To recite the prayer to St. Michael the Archangel.[27]
2. To mortify our eyes and avoid unhealthy daydreaming in order to avoid impurity.
3. To examine our conscience to see if we are not committing sins under the appearance of good. If there is a doubt, to seek the advice of a priest.

---

[27] See end of booklet.

THE DIVINE PEDAGOGY

# Tuesday of the Fifth Week after Epiphany

## God speaks to us

*Blessed are they who suffer persecution for justice' sake, for theirs is the kingdom of Heaven.*

—St. Matthew 5:10

## Meditation

In the government of the world, God brings good out of evil. Thus, for example, heresies, which in themselves are an evil, have allowed a deepening of certain points of Catholic doctrine.

Likewise, over the course of history, God has used the ambition or the malice of certain people in order to chastise others. Thus, under the emperor Titus, God used the ambition of the Romans to exercise His anger against His unfaithful people. "The ambition of the Romans was criminal, but the chastisements and the vengeance of the God were just."[28] In the same way, over the course of the history of the Church, God has used tyrants to raise up martyrs. Had there been no tyrants, there would have been no martyrs. Thus, martyrdom is a good which comes from an evil, from the malice of the wicked.

This outlook of God, who brings good out of evil, is the model we have to follow in our interaction with sinners. A given person of my acquaintance has an irritable temperament. He is impossible to deal with. He flies into a rage over nothing. In itself, that is an evil. But it is up to me to make a good come from it by my patience. This other person declares he is my enemy. It is up to me to take advantage of that situation to purify my own charity.

---

[28] Bourdaloue, *Complete Works*, II, p. 61.

St. Gregory goes so far as to say, "never, in the ordinary course of things, would a just man be perfect nor could he become perfect, if God, by the disposition of His providence, did not sometimes oblige him to live with sinners,"[29] because it is in the midst of adversity that God wills to purify us.

If we never had offenses or injustices to suffer, if we were never tried by backbiting or calumny, where would be the merit of our perseverance? How would we be able to judge the quality of our virtues?

O Lord Jesus, in seeing how Thou allowest this mixture of cockle and good seed for my sanctification, I desire from now on to bear with greater patience the defects of my neighbor.

## Prayer

O Lord God, I know that I need patience above all else, for in this life there are many trials.
*—Imitation of Christ*, III, Ch. 12

*Or:*

Lord, make possible for me by grace what is impossible to me by nature.
*—Imitation of Christ*, III, Ch. 19

## Thoughts

- Your troubles are but small in comparison with those who have suffered so much, whose temptations were so strong, whose trials so severe.
  *—Imitation of Christ*, III, Ch. 19

- God tolerates evil, but it is not without compensation nor without benefit for His Church.
  *—The Friend of Parish Clergy*, XI, p. 38

---

[29] *Ibid.*

## Resolutions

1. To recite a decade of the rosary for Christians throughout the world who are suffering persecution.
2. Not to shoot back an answer when someone makes us an unpleasant comment.
3. To offer our sufferings to God in order to make them meritorious.

THE PATIENCE OF GOD

# Wednesday of the Fifth Week after Epiphany

## God speaks to us

*[Do not pull out the weeds] lest in gathering the weeds you root up the wheat along with them.*
—Gospel of Sunday: St. Matthew 13:29

## Meditation

Why does God not intervene against the hostility, the wickedness, the hatred of the devil?

The servants want to pull up the weeds but their master refuses, telling them, *No, lest in gathering the weeds you root up the wheat along with them.* Here we have a glimpse of the divine heart of Jesus who wants to protect the wheat and so He waits patiently before pulling up the cockle. When the two plants are growing side by side, it is difficult to root one up and not the other. It is easier to distinguish the good and the bad spike than to separate the plants when they are still just in leaf. Moreover, the roots of the two plants tend to interlace, so that if one pulls out a stalk of cockle, there is a risk of pulling out a stalk of wheat with it. Finally, a person would have to walk through the field in order to get to the weeds, which would probably mean crushing stalks of wheat. So we see that it would be too risky an operation to want to pull out the cockle that is growing in among the wheat.

What is true of the field of wheat is true also of souls. Good and bad often live together, not only in the same town but even in the same house or in the same office. How could we separate them? How could we possibly give to each what he deserves? When we punish the wicked are we not also punishing the just? Likewise, when we reward the just, are we not at the same time rewarding the wicked, who do not deserve it? So it is not here below that the solution is to be found.

In addition, plants never change their nature, but men are not predetermined to be all their life either good or evil. At a certain point they may be the good grain of wheat, other times the cockle.

How many examples of cockle changing into good seed do we not see in Holy Scripture and in the history of the Church! If God had ripped out the weeds too soon, we would not have had a St. Mary Magdalen, nor even a St. Paul, or a St. Augustine. Therefore, if Our Lord does not step in immediately to stop the course of evil, it is because He is allowing sinners a chance to convert and come back to better dispositions.

## Prayer

Lord, in what can I trust in this life? And what is my greatest comfort on earth? Is it not Yourself, O Lord my God, whose mercy is limitless?
—*Imitation of Christ*, III, Ch. 59

*Or:*

O Lord, I see it clearly: Thy light and Thy strength do not fail me; what is lacking is my own perseverance. Grant me Thy patience.
—Fr. Gabriel, DI, II, pp. 32-33

## Thoughts

- Knowest thou not that the patience of God inviteth thee to repentance?
  —Rule of St. Benedict, Pr:37

- The man who has the happiness of remaining always patient and gentle is in his calmness a living image of God.
  —Curé of Ars, TD2, August 16

## Resolutions

1. To recite the fourth sorrowful mystery to ask for patience in a particular situation: at home, at work...
2. To overcome human respect in order to bear witness to our Faith at the next opportunity.
3. To send a letter or an email to a person far from the Faith, expressing our own joy at being a Catholic.

# THE HARVEST

# Thursday of the Fifth Week after Epiphany

## God speaks to us

*At harvest time, I will say to the reapers, "Gather up the weeds first and bind them in bundles to burn; but gather the wheat into my barn."*
—Gospel of Sunday: St. Matthew 13:30

## Meditation

The father of the family wants the weeds left in the field until the harvest. As they pull out the weeds, they might uproot the good grain. Yes, Our Lord is patient and He leaves sinners the time to convert.

But we could argue back that sinners do not all convert. It is true. Those sinners nonetheless enter the action of Providence. From the spectacle of iniquity triumphant, God raises up sublime virtues; from the persecution of the wicked, He gathers heroic sacrifices, merits which we would never acquire if life were calm; from the aggressions of error, He draws forth brilliant manifestations of truth.

For all of these reasons, we must have patience and wait for the last day, when God will render to each according to his works. That is the final lesson of the parable. *At harvest time, I will say to the reapers, "Gather up the weeds first and bind them in bundles to burn."* Thus we can see that the patience of God does not disarm His justice. The mercy which He shows today to sinners does not mean that they will remain unpunished if they do not convert.

So, may sinners not take advantage of that temporary leniency to plunge deeper into sin, but may they remember that the wrath of God will be all the greater for His having been patient longer. *Dies iræ, dies illa*, "that day will be a day of wrath!" Yes, a day is coming when the weeds and the good grain will be separated definitively. The just will be welcomed into the barn of the master, while the wicked are cast into the fire of Hell. The first will enjoy eternal life and the last will suffer eternal death.

When we are disconcerted at the apparent inaction of God, let us think of these reflections which Our Lord offers us in the Gospel of the weeds and the wheat, and let us do what depends on us to merit being welcomed into His barn, so as to sing forever His mercies in the blessed eternity of Heaven.

## Prayer

O King of awful majesty, who of Thy free gift savest them that are to be saved, save me, O fount of mercy!

Remember, O loving Jesus, 'twas for my sake Thou camest on earth: let me not, then, be lost on that day.

*—Dies Iræ*

*Or:*

O righteous awarder of punishment, grant me the gift of pardon before the reckoning-day.

*—Dies Iræ*

## Thoughts

- If you have not made any sacrifices, you will have nothing to harvest… A day is coming when we will find that nothing which we have done to gain Heaven has been too much.
  —Curé of Ars, TD2, March 5

- If we made God increase in our soul every day, think what confidence that would give us to appear one day before His infinite holiness!
  —Elizabeth of the Trinity, L 224

## Thursday of the Fifth Week after Epiphany

## Resolutions

1. To read and meditate on the prayer *Dies Iræ*[30] in order to draw down the mercy of God upon ourselves and upon sinners.
2. To wait for the right moment to practice fraternal correction, taking care not to forget about it!
3. To offer a sacrifice in a spirit of reparation for our sins.

---

[30] See end of booklet.

# THE WEEDS CAST INTO THE FIRE

# Friday of the Fifth Week after Epiphany

## God speaks to us

*Gather up the weeds first and bind them in bundles to burn.*
—Gospel for Sunday – St. Matthew 13:30

## Meditation

The weeds will be cast into the flames! What better moment for us to remember that there is fire not only on earth, but also in the next life? And beyond this material flame there is yet another fire: the fire of charity.

Earthly fire is the symbol of divine chastisements. Do we not see in the Old Testament Sodom and Gomorrah chastised by fire? Blasphemers and committers of sacrilege devoured by the flames? Has Our Lord not warned us in the Gospel that "every tree that is not bringing forth good fruit is to be cut down and thrown into the fire" (Mt. 3:10)? There is the fire of Hell—for Hell exists—an eternal fire which burns without consuming, torturing the soul as well as the body. Let us love to repeat the words of the *Dies Iræ*: *Ne perenni cremer igne*; Lord, "grant that I may not burn in the unquenchable fire." There is also the fire of purgatory where the poor souls suffer, for they do not see God and they burn for Him with longing.

Does not each one of us have the duty to struggle against wicked passions? Passions that enflame, devour, torment; unsatisfied desires, jealousies, fits of anger!

But if we possess the fire of divine love, we will be preserved from the fire of Hell, and the fire of Purgatory will be less violent. It is indeed of that fire of love that Jesus said, "I have come to cast fire on the earth and my one desire is that it spread, that it set all aflame" (*Cf.* Lk 12:49).

Love is a gift of God and sin is the refusal of love. Love is a gift of self to God and the sinner does not want to give himself... How we must foster and increase in ourselves the love of God, by prayer and the practice of the virtues!

Divine heart of Jesus, "burning furnace of charity," deign to place in my soul a spark of Thine own love, that I may always better love and serve God and my neighbor.

## Prayer

My prayers deserve not to be heard; but Thou art good: grant, in Thy kindness, that I may not burn in the unquenchable fire.

—*Dies Iræ*

Or:

Come, Holy Ghost, fill the hearts of Thy faithful and enkindle in them the fire of Thy love. Send forth Thy Spirit and they shall be created. And Thou shalt renew the face of the earth.

—Prayer to the Holy Ghost

## Thoughts

- In Hell, the fire will penetrate the body of the damned. It will make them a kind of burning furnace. It will devour the entrails and the heart of the reprobate in his chest, and his brain in his head; the blood will boil in his veins and the marrow in his bones.
  —St. Alphonsus Liguori, HDD, p. 49

- Just as there is an evil zeal of bitterness which separates from God and leads to Hell, so there is a good zeal which separates from evil and leads to God and life everlasting. Exercise this zeal with the most fervent love.
  —Rule of St. Benedict, 72:1-3

## Resolutions

1. To recite the act of charity[31] for those near to us, at home or at work.
2. To meditate for 10 minutes on Hell, its sufferings, its eternity, and to recite with attention the prayer, "O my Jesus, save us from the fires of Hell…"
3. To offer a sacrifice for the solace of a soul in Purgatory.

---

[31] See end of booklet.

# THE NECESSARY VIGILANCE

# Saturday of the Fifth Week after Epiphany

## God speaks to us

*Watch and pray, that you may not enter into temptation.*

—St. Matthew 26:41

## Meditation

In theology, we learn that God only dwells with sinners by the necessity of His being.

In our interaction with sinners, we have to imitate God's procedures. As we can see, God tolerates sinners. St. Augustine explains that it is only just that we tolerate them as well, because we ourselves have perhaps not always been faithful to God and people have had to tolerate us in the past. We should therefore act toward sinners as people had to act toward us when we were in sin. We must never forget our mistakes and our past sins, so that we may always be merciful toward those who stray from the right path.

"St. Augustine does not say that the society of sinners ought to be a subject of complacency for us, but an exercise of patience; that is to say that we should suffer their presence and not love it."[32] The tragedy is that, too often, habitual contact with people who do not have our ideas ends up by weakening the conviction of Catholics. Little by little, insensibly, Catholics let themselves be taken in by the trap of concession to the spirit of the world, whether by worldliness or liberalism. When we do not foster in ourselves the Catholic spirit by good readings, by profound prayer, by keeping company with people who are fully Catholic, we run the risk of losing our savor and of one day settling contentedly into a mediocre life.

---

[32] Bourdaloue, *Complete Works*, II, p. 55.

To avoid these pitfalls, we have to know that in some cases we should imitate now what Our Lord will do at the Last Judgment. We all know the old adage, "Tell me your company, and I will tell you what you are." Let us therefore always be prudent in our relationships with people who are not recommendable whether by morals or religion, and let us not hesitate to put a stop to those relationships which are occasions of sin for us.

O Mother of God, obtain for me the grace of constant vigilance so that I might advance more surely toward the eternal blessedness of Heaven.

## Prayer

O holy Child Jesus, who fled into Egypt to teach me not to face danger imprudently, I promise you no longer to be rash and always to flee those occasions that are dangerous for my salvation.
—St. Alphonsus Liguori, HDD, p. 33

*Or:*

O Jesus, who fled before Herod to teach me to flee from danger! Grant me to preserve my soul from wicked occasions, whatever the cost.
—St. Alphonsus Liguori, HDD, p. 55

## Thoughts

- Souls who seek the occasion of sin, who expose themselves to it willfully, Heaven does not protect, even if they pray.
—St. Alphonsus Liguori, HDD, p. 33

- To will to expose yourself to the occasion of sin is to will to damn yourself.
—St. Alphonsus Liguori, HDD, p. 55

## Resolutions

1 To examine our conscience in order to discern the principal obstacle to our union with God, and then to make appropriate resolutions.
2 To flee near occasions of sin. Specify them interiorly.
3 To be prudent in the choice of our friends.

# THE MUSTARD SEED

# Sixth Sunday after Epiphany

### God speaks to us

*The kingdom of Heaven is like a grain of mustard seed, which a man took and sowed in his field.*
—Gospel: St. Matthew 13:31

### Meditation

The man who sows the grain in the field is Our Lord. The grain of mustard seed, the smallest of all seeds—which grows to be the largest of the garden plants, and in Palestine becomes even a tree of six feet high, a tree that bears abundant fruit and gives shelter and food to the birds of heaven—that seed signifies the truth of the Gospel sown in the world. In the beginning, it was minuscule, nearly imperceptible, but thanks to the preaching of the apostles it has spread over all the earth.

This tree therefore represents the prodigious development of the Church from the 12 Apostles, in spite of all the obstacles encountered. Indeed, very rapidly, starting from nothing, the Church spread in an extraordinary manner throughout the entire world. Thus has she become that tree in which the birds of heaven love to build their nests, the birds of heaven being the spiritual souls who rise toward God through contemplation.

But what is true of the whole Church is true also of each one of our souls taken individually. In fact, certain Fathers of the Church have seen in the grain of mustard seed and in the leaven, the seed of sanctifying grace, which is imperceptible to the senses but which little by little produces fruits of grace and virtue, in ever more abundance.

When the water of baptism flows over the forehead of the little baby, the seed of grace is placed there, like the grain of mustard seed in the earth. The supernatural life does not then appear outwardly, but with time it is meant to grow, develop and spread to fullness in the bright sunshine, just like the mustard seed.

It is the smallest of all grains. Truly, this seed of the first grace is hidden, imperceptible, inaccessible to our gaze. But let the soul be faithful to it, let it cooperate with that grace by a right use of its freedom, and the soul will soon become that tree of the Gospel which presents to our eyes a beautiful harmony, a beautiful balance, a great majesty.

O my Jesus, I want to have a fruitful life, in answer to Thy desire: "So let your light shine before men, in order that they may see your good works and give glory to your Father in Heaven" (Mt. 5:16).

## Prayer

O Jesus, who have welcomed me as a member of Thy Mystical Body, grant that I may not live there as a stranger but that I may serve the good of all my brothers.

—Fr. Gabriel, DI, VI, p. 7

*Or:*

O Jesus, who offered Thyself without reserve for the salvation of the world, enkindle in my heart an ardent zeal for the salvation of souls.

—Fr. Gabriel, DI, VI, p. 3

## Thoughts

- Blessed tree [of the Catholic Church], I found Thee planted next to my cradle; Thy flowers charmed my childhood, Thy branches protected my youth, Thy fruits nourished my life; even merely to contemplate them, to study them, gives me strength.

  —*The Friend of Parish Clergy*, VI, p. 21

- Fear not, little flock... He who is pleased to take a tiny seed and make it a spreading tree has promised you the kingdom.

  —*The Friend of Parish Clergy*, VI, p. 22

## Resolutions

1 To recite a *Magnificat* in thanksgiving for the Faith received at baptism.
2 To offer to help around the house.
3 To tell the children the beginning of the history of the Church, which we find in the Acts of the apostles.

THE LEAVEN IN THE DOUGH

# Monday of the Sixth Week after Epiphany

## God speaks to us

*The kingdom of Heaven is like leaven, which a woman took and buried in three measures of flour, until all of it was leavened.*
—Gospel of Sunday: St. Matthew 13:33

## Meditation

Among the Jews, even more than in our country, it was the woman who prepared and baked the bread for the family, although there were already bakeries in Palestine. An image from His childhood certainly came to Our Lord's memory. Their life in Nazareth was poor, and many times had He seen His holy Mother make with her own hands the bread that was to nourish the Holy Family.

The *three measures* are even an allusion to a common practice in Israel. Apparently that was the amount of flour used to prepare the bread for some solemn festival.

So Our Lord often saw this very natural activity being carried out, and His penetrating gaze read there the divine secret that it symbolizes. Let us try then to discover the profound thought of Jesus and the purpose of this parable. What is signified by the leaven making the dough rise? Our Lord tells us: it is an image of the kingdom of Heaven.

The leaven is sanctifying grace, that grace made up of faith and charity. When it is incorporated into the human soul, it works deep and intimate effects, like the action of leaven in the flour.

As for the flour, it is the world. The leaven is small in volume and simple in nature but has astonishing properties. Scarcely is it mixed into a mass of flour when it begins pushing out from the center with extraordinary strength and energy. However voluminous that mass of flour, the leaven penetrates it, transforms it, makes it become like itself. The action of the leaven is performed without noise and more slowly or quickly depending on the place it is. Its action is gradual but tenacious; it is persevering, efficacious, victorious. The leaven raises up the dough, lightens it, expands it, gives it savor. It changes the flour entirely, both in shape and in substance. Nothing is left untouched by its influence.

To take only two aspects, we can say that the leaven transforms the dough and unifies it. Those are certainly two characteristics of divine grace in souls. Grace, indeed, transforms our soul to the depths and unifies it by fixing for it a single goal toward which all effort is meant to converge.

## Prayer

Grant me, O Lord, a simple heart, without duplicity nor detours; a heart which tends toward Thee with the simplicity of a child.
—Fr. Gabriel, DI, V, p. 107

*Or:*

Give support to my weakness, O Lord, so that I might attain the possession of Thy kingdom.
—Fr. Gabriel, DI, V, p. 114

## Thoughts

- It is always the leaven, or the grace of Jesus Christ, which rules the dough; which takes over, penetrates, seizes the earthly man, the man still fragile, sensual, animal, to turn him into a spiritual being, heavenly, divine.
—*The Friend of Parish Clergy*, VI, p. 39

- Let us not allow ourselves to be tainted or infected by any stale, insipid leaven of modern liberalism. Let us not become adulterated dough.
—*Friend of Parish Clergy*, VI, p. 39

## Monday of the Sixth Week after Epiphany

**Resolutions**

1. To recite the litany of humility.[33]
2. To beg God for the virtue which we would like to acquire or see increase in us.
3. To be more efficacious in our duty of state by avoiding what may distract us or prevent us from focusing deeply on our work.

---

[33] See end of booklet.

THE MISSIONARY LEAVEN

# Tuesday of the Sixth Week after Epiphany

## God speaks to us

*In this is my Father glorified, that you may bear very much fruit.*
—St. John 15:8

## Meditation

The leaven which is buried in the dough and causes it rise and swell, making the bread more airy and more appetizing, is the image of what the Christian ought to be in the world. This parable shows us in fact how Catholics, far from letting themselves be contaminated by the spirit of the world, should on the contrary labor for its conversion by being that leaven which little by little communicates its strength to all the dough. In such a way did the entire world cease to be pagan and become Christian.

It therefore falls to us to manifest the glory of our heavenly Father by developing to the fullest the gifts that we have received from God. Some have received more, others less, but we have all received the duty to make them bear fruit.

What should we do to develop our talents and become this great tree of the Gospel; to be, for those around us, the leaven in the dough?

First of all, we have to will it. God created us free and He does not do violence to our freedom. He respects it. He only gives Himself in proportion to our good will. So we should give ourselves to Our Lord with a generous movement of our will, so that He will work in us that transformation which is essentially the fruit of His grace. It is certainly not by pulling ourselves up by our bootstraps that we are going to become saints. God is the one who changes our hearts, He is the one who makes us better; but that slow and progressive transformation cannot happen without our cooperation.

Thus, the first disposition which allows God to act is a disposition of openness, of generosity. God knows better than we do what it is that we need. We must let Him act. Let us have confidence in Him. Let us not imitate that little child whose teacher asked him to compose a prayer in honor of the Sacred Heart and who wrote in all simplicity: "Most Sacred Heart of Jesus, have confidence in me." No, our confidence does not rest upon us, but upon God.

O my Jesus, help me to live habitually in a state of dependence upon Thee, and then to take the means to develop the talents which Thou hast confided to me. I promise Thee also to share with others my joy at being Catholic.

## Prayer

Teach me, Lord, to place at the service of the apostolate all of the talents which I have received from Thee.
—Fr. Gabriel, DI, VI, p. 81

*Or:*

Lord, grant that I may bring nearer to Thee all those who draw near to me.
—St. Francis de Sales, TD, July 8

## Thoughts

- We would like our prayer to be over quickly because we are anxious to get on with our work. We forget that prayer is what is most important in action. It is truly the grace of God which acts in our life, so prayer becomes very important in obtaining grace.
—Fr. Maximilian Kolbe, M, p. 131

- In truth, they are already great in the eyes of the Lord, who, by the example of their pious life, convert the hearts of those around them to the service of almighty God.
—St. Gregory the Great, TD, March 30

## Resolutions

1. To recite a decade of the rosary for the conversion of someone near or dear to us.
2. To set a good example whether at school or at work.
3. To read a chapter of the catechism for our own formation, or read the account of the beatitudes from November 1st in our missal.

MAGNANIMITY

# Wednesday of the Sixth Week after Epiphany

### God speaks to us

*Let your light shine before men, in order that they may see your good works and give glory to your Father in Heaven.*

—St. Matthew 5:16

### Meditation

In order to be the leaven in the dough, in order to become this great tree of the Gospel, let us be magnanimous. Magnanimity, or "greatness of soul," consists in cultivating the desire to undertake great things for God and for our neighbor. Let us therefore love God and our neighbor, and let us develop our qualities for the glory of our heavenly Father and the good of those around us.

Magnanimity does not consist in escaping from the world that surrounds us and dreaming of a marvelous world in which we play the leading role, as we see in certain films or read in certain novels. Magnanimity consists in recognizing the talents which God has given us in order to make them bear fruit.

It is false humility to despise our talents and it would be a serious mistake to bury them under pretext that they might lead us to vainglory or pride. Certainly, if we have a tendency to steal the glory of God by taking vanity from the good that we do, then we need to make an effort to correct ourselves, but that is no reason for just doing nothing.

Moreover, magnanimity goes hand in hand with prudence. The prudent man manages as best he can the talents which he has received. He knows his qualities and his limits and he acts accordingly.

And in any case, the magnanimous man leans on the grace of God to develop his gifts. He knows that it is the divine power which will have the last word in the gigantic combat which today is ranging the good against the forces of evil.

Yes, the magnanimous man knows that God will have the victory, but he knows that this victory will not take place without the cooperation of the faithful. This greatness of soul, this magnanimity, is what the world stands most in need of today. The world is so debased, so corrupt, that we need souls of conviction, souls of strength and of determination, to resist the forces of evil.

It could very well be that we find ourselves one day in a situation such that our only choice is to be heroes or to be traitors. Yet, heroism does not arise in a soul all of a sudden, from one day to the next. It is prepared by fidelity to daily duty.

O my Jesus, help me to be more faithful to my duty of state than I have been up until now, and to do all the good which Thou expectest of me.

## Prayer

O Lord, give me a noble heart, capable of undertaking great things for Thee.

—Fr. Gabriel, DI, V, p. 128

*Or:*

Lord, increase my confidence in Thy help; may it always give me the courage to begin again.

—Fr. Gabriel, DI, V, p. 150

## Thoughts

- Our weakness will always grow weary, but a great confidence and a great love soon make us spread our wings.
  —Fr. Gabriel, DI, V, p. 130
- The more complete becomes our confidence in God, the stronger will we be with the divine strength.
  —Fr. Gabriel, DI, V, p. 130

## Resolutions

1 To set to work doing first what is most disagreeable.

2 To remember the promises of Jesus Christ concerning Heaven.

3 To render some service to our neighbor which will make him happy.

# THE SPIRIT OF FAITH

# Thursday of the Sixth Week after Epiphany

## God speaks to us

*The just man lives by faith.*
—Epistle of St. Paul to the Galatians 3:11

## Meditation

To magnanimity, let us join the spirit of faith. Faith consists in believing in the truths which God has revealed to us. Thus, he who has faith believes in all the truths which God has revealed and which He teaches by His Church.

What we call the spirit of faith consists in living according to the principles of faith. It is faith lived in the day-to-day.

God wants us to live by faith. But that life is difficult for us because faith is a semi-darkness. The truths which God teaches us are not self-evident for us.

We therefore spontaneously look for another source for perceiving God and we naturally turn toward feelings. Since we cannot manage to see, we try to feel. It is true that sometimes, out of pity, God deigns to manifest Himself to us in a sensible manner. We are in front of the Blessed Sacrament and we have a good feeling. That is Our Lord "giving us sugar" to encourage us to love Him more and more. But we must not mistake the sugar for God Himself.

Since God is a pure spirit, the deepest union with Him cannot be a union of feelings, but a union of will. So on a practical level it is normal, it is perfectly natural, that we accept the sugar which God gives us; it is normal that we love such a feeling; but if we start reducing our spiritual life to trying to get sugar, we introduce a disorder which can be very damaging to our spiritual balance.

## Thursday of the Sixth Week after Epiphany

And so we encounter souls who, the minute they stop feeling anything, either abandon their exercises of piety, or else turn in on themselves and spend their time analyzing themselves to see if they still are in the state of grace or if they still have the Faith.

The remedy to all that morbid introspection, to that constant analysis of our states of soul, is to have our eyes toward God, it is the spirit of faith, which makes us believe in the personal love of Our Lord for us and then act accordingly.

Yes, Lord Jesus, I believe in Thy love for me. Thou hath shown it so clearly throughout Thy life and particularly during Thy painful Passion.

## Prayer

Give me, O Lord, that spirit of faith which will allow me to maintain myself in contact with Thee in the midst of any occupation or circumstance of my day.

—Fr. Gabriel, DI, III, p. 95

*Or:*

O my God, Trinity whom I adore, help me to forget myself entirely that I may be established in Thee, as still and as peaceful as if my soul were already in eternity.

—Elizabeth of the Trinity, *Prayer to the Trinity*[34]

## Thoughts

- True faith does not contradict by its manner of living what it affirms by its words.

  —St. Gregory the Great, TD, July 7

- A spirit of faith and of prayer in all we do is a tendency of the heart toward God and a simple gaze upon His holy will in order to conform ourselves to it.

  —Pauline Jaricot, TD, March 26

---

[34] Written on November 21st, 1904. *The Complete Works, Vol. 1: I Have Found God*, ICS Publications, 2014, p. 183.

## Resolutions

1. To recite and meditate on the act of faith, at the end of the booklet.

2. To make an act of adoration of the Holy Trinity three times a day. To read the second prayer above or the prayer of the angel of Fatima, at the end of the booklet.

3. To thank God for a great grace of my life and for a grace or blessing of this day.

# FR. LENOIR

# Friday of the Sixth Week after Epiphany

## God speaks to us

*We have believed in charity.*

—1st Epistle of St. John 4:16

## Meditation

Fr. Lenoir, military chaplain of an infantry regiment, said one day, "To bring God to the men of this regiment, I would give my life. I would give it for even one."[35]

At dawn on May 9th, 1917, stationed on the Eastern front, his regiment attacks a Germano-Bulgarian position which is then violently defended. The offensive proves impossible and the regiment is forced to retreat. The losses are enormous and many of the wounded remain on the battle field.

Fr. Lenoir does not pull back with the rest of the regiment. All morning, he runs or crawls throughout the field, crouches next to a dying man, then takes up his round again in the midst of the gunfire in order to carry out his priestly ministry.

At the beginning of the afternoon, he reaches a particularly dangerous sector. Soldiers who had taken shelter in holds made by sHells beg him not to go farther, where the terrain is open and the deadly machine-gun fire unceasing.

Fr. Lenoir moves back toward behind the lines, seeming to opt for prudence. Then he descends all the way to the fountain, stays there for a moment, motionless, recollected, and finally goes back toward the lines.

"A lieutenant stops him on the way, begs him not to attempt the impossible. Rather than giving up, he hands the officer the cane and the

---

[35] Paul Vigneron, *History of the Crises of the Modern French Clergy*, p. 188.

canteen that he is carrying over his shoulder and continues to advance, his face calm and grave… When he enters the zone open to enemy fire where lie the wounded and the dying, he kneels down one last time and finally slips into a field of green wheat… Lieutenant Gréau was watching the sector through his binoculars. He left this testimony: 'Around two o'clock in the afternoon, I saw a helmet in the wheat, at about 60 yards from my line. The helmet-cover stood out very distinctly behind the green stalks… and a machine gun fired immediately… [He remained there] motionless, his hands crossed over his chest, and his head slowly bowed.'"[36] Fr. Lenoir had completed his earthly ministry. The sacrifice was consummated.

## Prayer

Lord, grant that my love for Thee may not content itself with words, but prove itself by generous works.
—Fr. Gabriel, DI, VI, p. 186

*Or:*

Grant, O my God, that I may one day render even a small part of the great debts that I owe Thee!
—Fr. Gabriel, DI, VI, p. 189

## Thoughts

- With all my priestly heart, I beg you to ensure the eternal salvation of your souls by remaining faithful to Jesus Christ and to His law, by purifying yourselves of your sins, by uniting yourself to Him in Holy Communion as often as possible.
  —Fr. Lenoir to the soldiers of his regiment
- Courage. Suffering passes… In suffering, we merit Heaven, and Heaven is so beautiful!
  —Fr. Lenoir, L, p. 170

---

[36] *Ibid.*, p. 189.

## Resolutions

1. Make a spiritual communion (see end of booklet).
2. To offer a prayer for soldiers at war, and always to do so when passing before any kind of war memorial.
3. To help a person in difficulty, or to say an *Ave* for every homeless person you pass in the street, even if you have no alms to give.

# FR. DONCOEUR

# Saturday of the Sixth Week after Epiphany

## God speaks to us

*Charity impels us.*
—2nd Epistle of St. Paul to the Corinthians 5:14

## Meditation

Fr. Doncoeur, a military chaplain, was hesitating to venture all the way to the colonel's shelter to try to hear his confession. That officer had frequently and firmly declared that he wanted nothing to do with the sacraments. A bloody assault was expected the next day. We leave Fr. Doncoeur to tell us the tale of that 24th of September, 1915.

"We had seen four colonels of the division struck down in three days; around them, 4,000 dead! Under the bombardments of the last artillery preparation, with Fr. Ménard, we had heard the confessions of our comrades by the hundreds, trench by trench, battlement by battlement, and given them communion. Around seven in the evening, finishing the front of the regiment, we were passing in front of the HQ of the colonel. What should I do?... In the end... I walk down about 30 steps; I could have wished for 600. I was in front of the door. I knocked:

'Come in!'...

'Good evening, Colonel,' I said to him; 'I have just heard the confessions of our entire regiment.'

'I can see where you are heading with this.'

'You got it, Colonel, I am heading straight to the point—I want to end with you.'

Looking into his eyes, I realized that his soul was being shaken."

The officer made his confession and then, kneeling on the dirt floor, he received Holy Communion.

"When I gave him the host," continues Fr. Doncoeur, "I saw on that virile face, with its thick black mustaches, tears flowing down. I was very much moved. I knelt down, and then in a single movement we both embraced, and I spoke his thanksgiving for him..."[37] He died four days later, blown apart by a shell.

In contemplating such a priestly soul, how can we not be proud of our predecessors in the faith? May the example of Fr. Doncoeur multiply our own generosity. May we show forth as he did that beautiful virtue of magnanimity. So might we, like the mustard seed, become that great tree of the Gospel, or else be that leaven in the dough to spread the reign of Jesus and prepare His triumph.

## Prayer

Help me, Lord, to weep over my former iniquities, repel future temptations, correct my faults, and cultivate the virtues of my state in life.
—Clement XI, Universal Prayer

*Or:*

Grant, O Lord, that I may be ever-watchful to conquer my nature, cherish Thy grace, keep Thy laws, and merit salvation.
—Clement XI, Universal Prayer

## Thoughts

- As the priest is giving us absolution, we should be thinking of only one thing: that the blood of God is flowing over our soul to wash it, purify it and make it as beautiful as it was after baptism.
—Curé of Ars, TD2, April 17

- We have to spend more time asking for contrition than making our examination of conscience... We have to ask for real repentance.
—Curé of Ars, TD2, December 10

---

[37] Paul Vigneron, *History of the Crises of the Modern French Clergy*, p. 186.

## Resolutions

1 To recite the act of contrition slowly and attentively (see end of booklet).
2 To dare to bear witness to our Catholic Faith the next time an opportunity arises.
3 To make an act of preparation for death at the feet of Our Lady.

# Septuagesima

"The season of Septuagesima comprises the three weeks immediately preceding Lent. It forms one of the principal divisions of the liturgical year, and is itself divided into three parts, each part corresponding to a week: the first is called *Septuagesima*; the second, *Sexagesima*; the third, *Quinquagesima*.

"All three are named from their numerical reference to Lent, which, in the language of the Church, is called *Quadragesima*, that is, 40, because the great feast of Easter is prepared for by the holy exercises of 40 days. The words *Quinquagesima*, *Sexagesima*, and *Septuagesima*, tell us of the same great solemnity as looming in the distance, and as being the great object toward which the Church would have us now begin to turn all our thoughts, and desires, and devotion."[38]

During this liturgical period no *Alleluia* is sung, nor the *Gloria*, nor is the *Te Deum* sung at the night office. The Tract, which replaces the *Alleluia*, inspires the soul with sentiments of repentance, mixed with ardent supplication and great confidence. The violet color of the vestments indicates that we are gradually entering a time of sorrow and penance.

"The Christian, who would spend Septuagesima according to the spirit of the Church, must make war upon that false security, that self-satisfaction, which are so common to effeminate and tepid souls, and produce spiritual barrenness. It is well for them, if these delusions do not insensibly lead them to the absolute loss of the true Christian spirit. He that thinks himself dispensed from that continual watchfulness, which is

---

[38] Dom Guéranger, *The Liturgical Year: Septuagesima*, p. 1.

so strongly inculcated by our divine Master (Mk. 13:37), is already in the enemy's power. He that feels no need of combat and of struggle in order to persevere and make progress in virtue (unless he have been honored with a privilege, which is both rare and dangerous), should fear that he is not even on the road to that kingdom of God, which is only to be won by violence (Mt. 11:12). He that forgets the sins which God's mercy has forgiven him, should fear lest he be the victim of a dangerous delusion (Ecclus. 5:5). Let us, during these days which we are going to devote to the honest unflinching contemplation of our miseries, give glory to our God, and derive from the knowledge of ourselves fresh motives of confidence in Him, who, in spite of all our wretchedness and sin, humbled Himself so low as to become one of us, in order that He might exalt us even to union with Himself."[39]

---

[39] *Ibid.*, p. 14.

# THE INVITATIONS OF GOD

# Septuagesima Sunday

## God speaks to us

*The kingdom of Heaven is like a householder who went out early in the morning to hire laborers for his vineyard.*

—Gospel: St. Matthew 20:1

## Meditation

God has never ceased inviting souls to find their happiness in Him. Immediately after our first parents had been exiled from the garden of Eden, God promised them a savior, moving them to cling to the virtue of hope. Next, in the time of Noah, He used a rainbow to express the covenant which He willed to contract with us. Then He renewed His promise to Abraham, His servant, and assured him of a long posterity as a reward for his fidelity. After Abraham, there was Moses, who received a new blessing when God communicated to him the Tables of the Law. Then came the prophets to remind Israel of that covenant and to invite the members of the chosen people to remain faithful to their promises.

Yet God, who never ceases to love man with an infinite love, sought to contract with us a covenant even more pure, more profound, more irrevocable than the previous, to dissipate the darkness still enveloping His people. He invented a wondrous means of doing so, one which we would never have been able to imagine; one which floods our intellect with astonishment and ought to fill our hearts with love. That means would be the sacrifice of His own Son. Yes, "God so loved the world that He gave His only-begotten Son, that those who believe in Him may not perish, but may have life everlasting" (Jn. 3:16). And this Incarnation of the Word was to take place at the 11th hour, that is to say, it was to take place in the fullness of time.

Thus did Our Lord Himself come to pay that debt which we had contracted by our sins, and thereby inspire us to love Him even more and never again to leave Him.

So we see that from the very first hour of the day, God has not ceased to call workers to His vineyard. It is true of the history of humanity and it is equally true of the life of each one of us. The heavenly Father never stops inviting us to work in His vineyard. He is constantly seeking to touch our souls in order to make us grow in His love.

Help me, O Jesus, to be vigilant, to be attentive to the invitation of Your heavenly Father, and so bear fruit in abundance.

## Prayer

Bless, O Lord, this new liturgical period which begins today. May I let myself be penetrated by its spirit and so dispose myself, with Your help, to a serious reform of my spiritual life.

—Fr. Gabriel, DI, II, p. 5

*Or:*

O my Lord, I wish no longer to oppose any resistance to Your invitation. Grant that this day may sound for me the decisive hour of a response to Your call full of generosity and perseverance.

—Fr. Gabriel, DI, II, p. 6

## Thoughts

- Observe your way of living, brothers, and see if you are already God's workers. May each one examine what he does, and ask himself if he is working well in the vineyard of the Lord.

    —St. Gregory the Great, TD, May 7

- He who in this life seeks his own interests has not yet come into the vineyard of the Lord.

    —St. Gregory the Great, TD, November 19

## Resolutions

1. To arrive at Mass at least a few minutes early.
2. To be particularly recollected in order to be attentive today to the inspirations of the Holy Ghost.
3. To thank God for having sent His Son to redeem us.

# THE TWO ROADS

# Monday of Septuagesima

### God speaks to us

*I have set before you life and death, blessing and cursing.*
—Deuteronomy 30:19

### Meditation

In Holy Scripture, God very often speaks about two roads, one road that leads to Heaven, the other that leads to Hell.

Many people draw the conclusion that human life has a line down the middle. They have the impression that on one side you have the good, those who are faithful, who love God with all their heart, and on the other side you have the wicked or the ignorant, and there are many of these today. Some of them are hostile to the true God and others are merely indifferent. That impression is not entirely false, but we often forget that people pass from one side of the line to the other over the course of their human life. People can change camps. We are not predetermined to stay in one or the other.

How do we explain all this back and forth over the course of a human life? We can explain the falls by man's penchant for evil or for unbridled pleasure. To commit evil, all we have to do is let ourselves give in to our bad tendencies. Alas, we all bear the consequences of original sin. We are attracted by one thing one day, and by the contrary the day after. That inconstancy can easily make us fall into lukewarmness and infidelity, one day or another, if we let ourselves give in to it.

As long as we are here on earth, we are capable of forgetting the promised land. It is easy to take wrong steps that little by little draw us away from the goal, and so we see how certain children can have fallen to where they are, or certain adolescents, or certain adults, and even certain elderly people. Consequently, whatever our age, whatever our degree of virtue, we should not ever cry victory.

On the other hand, we should not ever despair of the salvation of souls. On a regular basis, priests are the witness of magnificent conversions, spectacular returns to God. It is very encouraging. And there is no natural explanation. Naturally, man can fall, he can succumb, but he cannot, of himself, return to God. Such a conversion requires a powerful grace. Our Lord never stops giving that grace at every hour of the day, as the parable of the vineyard shows us.

O my Jesus, I wish to seize hold of Thy grace of conversion and sanctification, relying on the help of my guardian angel. I promise Thee to be docile to his inspiration.

## Prayer

Show me, O Lord, the narrow path which leads to true life, to union with Thee.

—Fr. Gabriel, DI, II, p. 18

*Or:*

O Father who art in heaven, deliver us from evil.

—Fr. Emmanuel, M, p. 85

## Thoughts

- I have never yet found in the words of Our Lord that anyone has entered paradise joking around, acting foolish and following his inclinations, but everyone has entered by the narrow gate, and the Lord Himself did not go in by any other way.

  —St. Jane de Chantal, R, p. 34

- Narrow is the gate that leads to life and to pass through it, one must know how to conduct oneself attentively in every action and with wise discretion. He who carelessly goes his own way and follows his own will forbids himself entry by the narrow gate.

  —St. Gregory the Great, TD, September 15

## Resolutions

1. To look for the principal obstacle hindering me from rising toward God right now, and to see how to overcome it.
2. To say a rosary for the conversation of a great sinner.
3. To thank God for having kept me alive.

# WORK AS A CHASTISEMENT

# Tuesday of Septuagesima

### God speaks to us

*Why do you stand here all day idle? ... Go you also into my vineyard."*
—Gospel of Sunday: St. Matthew 20:6, 8

### Meditation

The father of the family says to the workers of the 11th hour: *Why do you stand here all day idle?... Go you also into my vineyard.* This question and this command may not seem at first seem to concern us, but in fact they are well worth our stopping to reflect a moment, because work is closely bound up with the purification of our souls.

Work is necessary for all men as a chastisement for sin, as we see in the curse that God placed upon Adam: "In the sweat of thy face shalt thou eat bread" (Gen. 3:19). And the book of Ecclesiasticus makes it clear that "great labor is created for all men" (Ecclus. 40:1).

The result of original sin was death, but also the laborious, painful, unpleasant character of work. Just as death affects all men since the sin of our first parents, likewise work has become something punishing for all men. Previously the earth offered delicious fruits of its own bounty that Adam and Eve could enjoy without the least difficulty, for their greater pleasure, but today the earth only yields man its fruit through his laborious effort.

So there are two aspects to remember. Work is a law for all men and its unpleasant character is the consequence of sin. That is why idleness, meaning willful laziness, is such a grave offense in the eyes of God. In the words of St. Ambrose, "Idleness is a kind of second revolt of the creature against his God."[40] The first was the sin of Adam and Eve, the second is our refusal to endure the punishment due to sin.

---

[40] St. Ambrose, quoted by Bourdaloue, *Complete Works*, II, p. 82.

We need to acknowledge our condition as sinners and then embrace with zeal and even with eagerness this law of work, which allows us to heal our disorders and to carry out here on earth the punishment that our sins would merit in Purgatory.

Yes, Lord Jesus, I desire from now on to work with ardor, in a spirit of penance.

## Prayer

Glorious St. Joseph, pattern of all who are devoted to toil, obtain for me the grace to toil in the spirit of penance, in order thereby to atone for my many sins.

—St. Pius X

*Or:*

Help me, Lord, to deplore my past sins, to overcome my temptations in the future, to correct my vicious tendencies, and to practice the virtues of my state in life.

—Clement XI, Universal Prayer

## Thoughts

- The Christian takes up his work in a spirit of penance and in view of satisfying God, because he knows very well that it is the first punishment for his sin.
  —Bourdaloue, CW, II, p. 82
- Let us embrace with generosity the work which the Lord offers us: nothing should appear to us too difficult, if it means saving souls.
  —Fr. Gabriel, DI, II, p. 5

## Resolutions

1. To recite our rosary in reparation for our sins.
2. To offer the difficulties of our work in expiation for our sins.
3. To set to work right away and bring to completion whatever we undertake, starting first with the essential.

# WORK AS A REMEDY

# Wednesday of Septuagesima

### God speaks to us

*Thorns and thistles shall the earth bring forth to thee.*

—Genesis 3:18

### Meditation

The burdensome character of work, which is first a consequence of sin, is also a remedy for sin. To encourage ourselves to accept this law of work, let us remember that it does not date from original sin. Only its unpleasantness dates from the fall of Adam.

God has never sinned, yet He presents Himself to us as a craftsman. From the very first page of Scripture, God reveals Himself to us as the artisan *par excellence*. Let us admire the heavenly Father who draws beings out of nothingness, one after another, assigning to each one a very specific place and role. He carries out His work in stages but every being is created in a simple act: "For He spoke, and they were made" (Ps. 148:5). The ease with which God brings to completion what He has determined is an invitation for us to keep our promises, to keep our professional commitments.

When God settled Adam in the earthly paradise, He asked him to work, also. Genesis tells us that "the Lord God took man, and put him into the paradise of pleasure, to dress it, and to keep it" (Gen. 2:15). But as we have said, it is only since original sin that work has become burdensome: "In the sweat of thy face shalt thou eat bread" (Gen. 3:19), *thorns and thistles shall the earth bring forth to thee*; but the law remains: "You will labor the earth."

"The world of the Gospel is likewise a world of laborers. St. Joseph exercises the trade of a carpenter, and the apostles were fishermen. Let us remember the scene where St. Peter says, 'the whole night we have toiled and have taken nothing' (Lk. 5:5). We can see very well that he did not remain idle."[41] This law of work is likewise inscribed in the parables, that of the workers in the vineyard, but also that of the sower, of the good shepherd, or else of the watchful servant.

Did not Jesus Himself spend the greater part of His life working in St. Joseph's carpentry shop? So much so that His neighbors would say, "Is this not Jesus, the son of Joseph the carpenter, whom we know very well?" (*Cf.* Jn. 6:42)

I promise You, O my Jesus, to embrace generously the law of work, convinced that it will preserve me from many temptations and many falls.

## Prayer

Lord Jesus, teach us to work without seeking for rest, to give without seeking any reward except that of knowing that we are doing Thy holy will.

—St. Ignatius of Loyola

*Or:*

St. Joseph, model of workers, pray for us.

## Thoughts

- Our great defense against the unruliness of the passions and the disorders of sin is industrious, persevering application to work.
  —Bourdaloue, CW, II, p. 84

- God will work with you, in you and for you and your work will be followed by consolation.
  —St. Francis de Sales, TD, May 10

---

[41] *The Catholic Family*, Clovis, 2011, p. 52.

## Resolutions

1 To recite the fourth sorrowful mystery.

2 To meditate for 10 minutes on the reward of Heaven, to encourage ourselves to work well.

3 To be a model of virtue in our school, in our university or in our work environment, avoiding two pitfalls: that of vainglory or ostentation; and that of false shame before our neighbor.

# THE DANGERS OF IDLENESS

# Thursday of Septuagesima

## God speaks to us

*Send your servant to work that he be not idle: for idleness hath taught much evil.*

—Ecclesiasticus 33:28-29

## Meditation

"Idleness is the mother of all vices." This saying is definitely founded on reality, and Holy Scripture is filled with examples that confirm it.

Let us look at the Hebrews. As long as they were marching through the desert, they stayed relatively faithful, but when Moses went to climb Mount Sinai and left them on their own, they found themselves with nothing to do. The Hebrew people then fell into idolatry, going so far as to forge a golden calf, and then, as Holy Scripture says, "the people sat down to eat and drink, and rose up to play" (Ex. 32:6). So the Hebrews began feasting and celebrating and then they fell into all kinds of disorders.

Let us look at King David. As long as he was busy directing his country and fighting its enemies, he remained faithful, but when he went home to rest, the temptation of the flesh assailed him and he fell. And the great King Solomon! All of his life, he had been truly exemplary. People came to him from far away to ask for advice because of his wisdom. But as soon as he withdrew from ruling and started trying to enjoy the kingly life a little more, he let himself be corrupted by luxurious living and in the end he, too, fell into idolatry.

We could cite other examples, but these are enough to show the dangers of idleness.

It is especially during vacation that idleness is a danger for us. And so, during these periods, let us avoid both an obsession for leisure and an obsession for the body. Our body, which St. Francis of Assisi baptized "brother donkey," needs leisure in order to be a more faithful servant of our soul, but let us take care not to grant it more than necessary or it will be constantly clamoring for more.

We have to beware of the pleasure of a certain ease that drains our vitality; the pleasure of bad reading, of bad films, of certain music, certain dances, which defile our soul; the pleasure of laziness which gives rise to many a moral misery.

Let us know how to relax in order to avoid burn-out, but in the choice of our relaxation let us energetically avoid anything contrary to our dignity as a child of God.

## Prayer

Jesus, may any joy without Thee be burdensome for me and may I not desire anything else besides Thee. May all work delight me when done for Thy sake and may all repose not centered in Thee be ever wearisome for me.

—St. Thomas Aquinas

*Or:*

St. Joseph, father and protector of virgins, preserve me from all stain, pure in mind and heart and chaste in body, that I may constantly serve Jesus and Mary in perfect purity.

—Prayer to obtain purity

## Thoughts

- Idleness is the enemy of the soul.

  —Rule of St. Benedict, 48:1

- It is dangerous to keep idle, whether in body or mind: for just as the earth, however good it be, will produce thorns and thistles if it is left fallow, so also our soul cannot stay long in repose and idleness without feeling some passions or temptations that carry it toward evil.

  —St. Vincent de Paul, TD2, March 23

## Resolutions

1. To identify and avoid the various wastes of our time: telephone, internet, empty or mind-numbing books...
2. To offer spontaneously to help around the house.
3. To make a firm and precise resolution to avoid inappropriate forms of leisure.

# THE DAILY SCHEDULE

# Friday of Septuagesima

### God speaks to us

*I do always the things that are pleasing to Him.*

—St. John 8:29

### Meditation

We have various obligations depending on our role in society, and it is not rare that we neglect certain of our duties and let ourselves be absorbed by others...or by leisure...

We can fail in some of our duties simply because we are disorganized, but certain other activities we do sometimes neglect deliberately because we find them distasteful.

So the first question we have to ask ourselves is this: Among our duties, do we not have a tendency to put too much emphasis on one aspect, to the detriment of some other?

Once we have made an inventory of our duties, we have to prioritize our activities, sifting what seems urgent from what is really important, and giving an absolute priority to what is important. That will help us to see where best to start and what time to dedicate to each activity.

And so if we wish our life to be more fruitful and effective, it is good to reflect on the way we spend the precious time which God gives us for working out our salvation.

Too many people let themselves be caught in the two-sided trap of overwork and idleness. So it is important to reflect on the means of avoiding this double pitfall.

The means is simple and it is within everybody's grasp: it is a daily schedule. A daily schedule that is well made, well structured, can help us bring more peace into our life, more serenity and more effectiveness.

For there are two ways of living: allowing the events of the day to carry us along as the various occupations arise one after the other, or else guiding those events by determining the place and the time for every occupation. And there is no doubt that this second solution is the better and the more effective of the two.

With a daily schedule that is well thought-out, we truly conform our will to the will of God and we run much less of a risk of sacrificing the essential to the secondary, the important to the trivial.

Help me, Lord Jesus, always to organize the broad lines of my days, to plan a time for everything, to be always occupied with something and to avoid not only idleness but overwork, both of which are harmful to my balance and to my spiritual life.

## Prayer

Ah! *Be it done unto me according to Thy word*. O my Mother, may my heart, lost in yours, have no other movement, no other will, no other love than the good pleasure of my divine Master.

—St. Bernadette, W, p. 373

*Or:*

O my Jesus, be my strength and my virtue!

—St. Bernadette, W, p. 369

## Thoughts

- Arrange and ordain all things that all may do their work without justifiable murmuring.

    —Rule of St. Benedict, 41:5

- Let us serve God well today; God will see to tomorrow. Let each day bear its own concerns, for the God who reigns today will reign tomorrow.

    —St. Francis de Sales, TD, January 10

## Resolutions

1 To work with order, avoiding wastes of time.

2 To begin our work with what is most contrary to our inclinations.

3 To make a schedule for the coming week and dare to eliminate the inessential.

# VIGILANCE AND CONFIDENCE

# Saturday of Septuagesima

## God speaks to us

*Many are called, but few are chosen.*
—Gospel for Sunday: St. Matthew 20:16

## Meditation

In the spiritual life, there are two pitfalls to be avoided: presumption on the one hand; discouragement on the other. The man who is too sure of himself, who has too much confidence in himself, is showing presumption. On the contrary, the man who is fearful, timorous, slips easily into discouragement.

Sad to say, we tend to vacillate between one and the other. When things are going smoothly, we tend to count too much on ourselves, be too satisfied with ourselves. When difficulties arise, we tend to lack perseverance and we fall into the trap of discouragement. So, to help us find a balance, God willed to show us on the one hand that we have not yet earned Heaven, and on the other hand, all is not necessarily lost just because for a time we have been following the wrong path.

It is therefore this double lesson of vigilance and confidence that the Church gives us through the texts of last Sunday's Mass. In the Gospel, Jesus clearly states that *many are called, but few are chosen*. So the majority do not choose the path to Heaven. And if that is true for the history of mankind in general, how much more true is it today. Let us therefore strive to be among the number of the elect!

It is our natural tendency to want an easy little life here below and to avoid effort, at the risk of falling into mediocrity. To help us avoid this pitfall, God has put us on our guard against the danger of letting ourselves be drawn down the slope of ease, onto the path of the greater number. He has invited us on the contrary to work with energy and determination and to win Heaven by our generosity.

## Saturday of Septuagesima

Lord Jesus, I take seriously the warning which Thou hast given in the Gospel, telling us that *many are called, but few are chosen*, and I wish to answer Thy call by working generously in Thy vineyard so as to earn the wages that Thou hast promised, namely, the happiness of Heaven.

## Prayer

O Lord Jesus, do not allow me to give in to discouragement at the constant return of my selfish tendencies and at the never-ending battle that I have to wage against them. Make me truly understand that, if I want to convert totally to Thee, I can never be indulgent with my weaknesses, with my sins, with my selfishness, with my self-love.
— Fr. Gabriel, DI, II, p. 88

*Or:*

My God, give me perseverance in the battle against my faults.
— St. Alphonsus Liguori, HDD, p. 311

## Thoughts

- Watch, then, praying at all times, that you may be accounted worthy to escape all these things that are to be, and to stand before the Son of Man.
  — St. Luke 21:36

- There is nothing which offends God so much as to despair of His mercy.
  — Curé of Ars, TD1, January 8

## Resolutions

1 To recite the litany of humility, meditating on the words.[42]

2 Not to let ourselves be drawn down the path of the greater number.

3 Never to give up on prayer nor be discouraged after our sins, but to set off again on the right foot after a good act of contrition.[43]

---

[42] See end of booklet.
[43] See end of booklet.

# GOD IN NATURE

# Sexagesima Sunday

## God speaks to us

*The heavens show forth the glory of God.*

—Psalm 18:2

## Meditation

The word of God is like a seed that is able to produce abundant fruit. This divine word is not only Holy Scripture but also nature itself, if we know how to contemplate it.

When we read the lives of the saints, we see them so eager to know God that everything in their life brought them back to Him. Thus they had the conviction that God speaks to us through creation. And nature really is a means of discovering God. It teaches us to know Him.

Many psalms invite us to see the mark of God in nature. The holy King David sang it in these words: *The heavens show forth the glory of God.* This verse offers us a glimpse into the contemplative soul of the Psalmist. As he stood admiring nature, what he saw was a manifestation of the glory of God.

In our day we ought to have an even greater admiration for nature because of the technical progress that allows us to discover even more aspects of the universe. For example, we are now able to count hundreds of billions of galaxies. Such a multitude is a proof of the greatness and power and generosity of God. By this example, we see that God is not miserly in His gifts. When He gives, He gives in profusion.

In speaking of all the beings that compose this beautiful nature, David specifically says that "their sound hath gone forth into all the earth: and their words unto the ends of the world" (Ps. 18:5). A person may not be a scholar or even know how to read, but he can still understand the language of nature. Everyone can. All we have to do is open our eyes. Yet we must know how to look, and this knowing how to look may be what modern man is most lacking.

Man today is often cut off from nature, living most of his life in the artificial atmosphere of cities, and he has forgotten how to look, he has forgotten how to admire. It is truly a pity. And so let us seek God in creation, like St. Francis of Assisi or, closer to us, St. Theresa of the Child Jesus and Elizabeth of the Trinity.

Yes, Lord Jesus, I wish to follow the example of the saints and admire this beautiful nature which You have created, and to render You worthy thanksgiving.

## Prayer

Lord, I feel in my heart the need to offer Thee thanks for all Thy benefits and to proclaim Thy ineffable goodness, to the glory of Thy name.
—Pauline Jaricot, TD, June 4

*Or:*

My God, I adore Thee as my first beginning, I long for Thee as my last end, I praise Thee as my constant benefactor, I call upon Thee as my loving protector.
—Clement XI, Universal Prayer

## Thoughts

- All nature seems so full of God to me: the wind blowing in the tall trees, the little birds singing, the beautiful blue sky, everything speaks to me of Him.
—Elizabeth of the Trinity, L 236

- How great is this nature that Thou hast made, my God, and how beautiful! What sweetness it is to stand before it and lift our souls toward Heaven.
—Elizabeth of the Trinity, P 9[44]

---

[44] In the French edition of the Complete Works, *Œuvres Complètes*, Cerf, 1991, p. 930.

## Resolutions

1. To recite a *Magnificat* in thanksgiving for the marvels of creation.
2. To take the time to admire nature the next time we make an outing, and to see there a reflection of the beauty and the greatness and the infinite goodness of God.
3. To teach the children to respect nature as the work of God.

## ORDER IN THE UNIVERSE

# Monday of Sexagesima

### God speaks to us

*And God said: Let the earth bring forth the living creature in its kind, cattle and creeping things, and beasts of the earth, according to their kinds… And God saw that it was good.*

—Genesis 1:24-25

### Meditation

If we know how to discover God in nature, we will be able to draw lessons for our daily life.

David, after gazing on nature with admiration, turns and exalts the Law of God, and Bossuet in his commenting on this psalm (Ps. 18) gives us the reason.[45] He shows us the connection between the praise of nature and the praise of the divine Law. He tells us that the holy king, having contemplated the marvels of nature, was led to consider the reasons for that harmony, the reasons for that splendid balance which he so admired. And he came to the conclusion that nature is so beautiful, the world is so admirable, only because of the Law of God which the creatures not endowed with reason all obey.

If the stars refused the laws of nature, if the sun ceased to obey the laws of nature, we can only imagine what the consequences would be. But because the stars respect the Law of God, because the sun is docile to God's commands, we are able to admire the order that rules over them.

In this way, the elements of nature are an invitation for us to follow the Law of God in our turn. If we know how to be faithful to the Law of God, we will rediscover that order in ourselves, that harmony, that same balance which we contemplate in nature. Yes, nature is beautiful, even if there seem to be shadows in the picture.

---

[45] Bossuet, *Oratorical Works*, I, pp. 309 ff.

Indeed, certain animals, far from being objects of admiration, are rather for man objects of horror. It is true. And yet, ferocious or dangerous animals have their place in nature and God also speaks to us through them. The sight of them reminds us of the sin of our first parents, reminds us of the consequences of their disobedience. This consideration moves us to restrain our disordered passions.

There exist therefore many lessons to be drawn from nature, whether from the wonders that we discern there or the harmful elements that we encounter.

## Prayer

Provided that Thy will be done in me, in all of Thy creatures, I desire nothing more, my God.

—Fr. de Foucauld

*Or:*

O Jesus, the most obedient of all, make me understand the value of obedience.

—St. Alphonsus Liguori

## Thoughts

- Contemplate this beautiful structure of the world; see that accord and that harmony: is there anything more beautiful or better fashioned than this great and splendid edifice? It is because there the will of God has been faithfully observed.

  —Bossuet, OW, I, p. 331

- If even bodily creatures receive such adornment because they obey the decrees of God, how great will be the beauty of intelligent natures when they are ruled by His ordinances!

  —Bossuet, OW, I, p. 331

## Resolutions

1. To meditate for 10 minutes on the order of the universe.
2. To obey promptly and joyfully.
3. To accept daily vexations and unexpected turns of events, such as the weather, without complaint.

# NATURE: A SCHOOL OF LIFE

# Tuesday of Sexagesima

## God speaks to us

*Look at the birds of the air: they do not sow, or reap, yet your heavenly Father feeds them.*

—St. Matthew 6:26

## Meditation

"Creatures do not simply make us know God, they also give us precious teaching to govern our life."[46]

God Himself, in Holy Scripture, points to the manner of living of the animals as an example to encourage us to develop our talents. Thus, for example, it is written in the book of Proverbs, "Go to the ant, O sluggard, and consider her ways, and learn wisdom: which, although she hath no guide, nor master, nor captain, provideth her meat for herself in the summer, and gathereth her food in the harvest. Or go find the bee and learn of her how she loveth her work" (Prov. 6:6-8).[47] But, all in developing our talents, we also have to trust in divine Providence. *Look at the birds of the air*, Our Lord tells us; *they do not sow, or reap, yet your heavenly Father feeds them.*

Moreover, nature not only invites us to live correctly here below, but even helps us to believe in the supernatural truths that Our Lord has revealed to us. Thus, for example, Jesus Christ confirmed our hope in the resurrection of the body. Yet, this reality is also prefigured in nature. Wheat, for example, which rots in the earth in order to produce more abundant, more perfect seeds, gives us a glimpse into the resurrection of the body. Likewise the vine, which appears dried out in winter and recovers its foliage in the springtime, offers us material for reflection

---

[46] St. John Chrysostom, *Complete Works*, V, p. 180, commentary on Psalm 110.
[47] As quoted by St. John Chrysostom, *ibid.*, p. 181.

on the great mystery of the resurrection. Thus, the cycle of plant life strengthens our hope in the future resurrection.

God speaks therefore through nature and teaches us to discern there what He expects of us today. But for that we have to open the eyes of our body and look on nature with our faith.

Lord Jesus, give me the grace of that contemplative gaze upon nature which was the secret of so many saints, in order that I might always rise from the creature to the Creator. I thank You, my God, for the marvels of creation.

## Prayer

Glorious St. Joseph, pattern of all who are devoted to toil, obtain for me the grace to toil conscientiously, putting devotion to duty before my own inclinations; to labor with thankfulness and joy, deeming it an honor to employ and to develop, by my labor, the gifts I have received from Almighty God.

—St. Pius X

*Or:*

My Father, I commend myself to Thee, I give myself to Thee, I leave myself in Thy hands. My Father, do with me as Thou wilt. Whatever Thou chooseth to do with me, I thank Thee; I accept everything.

—Fr. de Foucauld

## Thoughts

- Death, life, illness, health—everything happens to us by order of Providence.

  —St. Vincent de Paul, TD1, January 21

- Even just seeing a person, we know if she is pure. Her eyes have an air of candor and modesty that raises us toward God.

  —Curé of Ars, W, p. 120

## Tuesday of Sexagesima

# Resolutions

1 To work generously with joy and perseverance.
2 To live the present moment under the eyes of God.
3 To respect our body, temple of the Holy Ghost, by decent apparel.

## GOD IN HOLY SCRIPTURE

# Wednesday of Sexagesima

### GOD SPEAKS TO US

*God, who at sundry times and in divers manners spoke in times past to the fathers by the prophets, last of all in these days has spoken to us by His Son.*
—Epistle of St. Paul to the Hebrews 1:1-2

### MEDITATION

God speaks through nature, but He also and especially speaks to us through Holy Scripture, where He reveals Himself to man. *To reveal* means "to raise the veil." To make Himself known to us, God has taken away the veil that kept Him hidden.

This revelation begins with Genesis. God made Himself known to Adam and Eve, with whom He converses in the evening breeze. Then, after original sin, He made Himself known to Noah, to Abraham, to Moses, and to all the prophets.

In His pedagogy, only little by little did God reveal Himself to men. Not until the coming of Our Lord would this Revelation be whole and entire, for God spoke to us through Our Lord Jesus Christ, true God and true man. He made Himself known to us by His Son, who is equal to Him in all things. What a mystery! And what progress also can we make in the knowledge of God!

God has shown to us the mysteries of His inner life, as well as the mysteries of our origin and our destiny. He has taught us that there are three Persons in God: the Father, the Son and the Holy Ghost. We have discovered that the second Person of the Blessed Trinity took a nature like our own to deliver us from sin. This is the mystery of the Incarnation and the mystery of the Redemption.

God warned us next that life on earth is not made for enjoying, but for meriting: meriting Heaven, meriting to live eternally the blessed life of the angels through the vision of His majesty.

He has also given us our marching orders in order to get to Heaven, in other words, His commandments and those of His Church. And He threatened with eternal fire those who refuse to follow His commandments: "He who believes... shall be saved, but he who does not believe shall be condemned" (Mk 16:16). And to help us to remain faithful, He has given us the help of prayer and the sacraments.

That is what Revelation contains: the word of God, *Verbum Dei*.

Lord Jesus, since Thou hast taken the means of coming down from Heaven to earth to teach me the divine mysteries, help me to contemplate them already here below and so merit to enjoy goods that are eternal, in the life to come.

## Prayer

Most wise St. Joseph, obtain for me the taste for Christian knowledge.
—St. Alphonsus Liguori, HDD, p. 72

*Or:*

O God, who didst instruct the hearts of the faithful by the light of the Holy Ghost, grant that by the same Spirit we may be truly wise and ever rejoice in His consolation. Through the same Jesus Christ Our Lord.
—Prayer to the Holy Ghost

## Thoughts

- It is not enough to hear this divine word; we have to keep it; and to keep it, we have to chew on it. What does it mean to "chew on it," if not to meditate on it?
  —St. Francis de Sales, TD, October 18

- Let us strive to meditate on the word of God, so as to be nourished by it.
  —St. Benedict, TD, August 11

## Resolutions

1 To make a spiritual communion (see end of booklet).
2 To read with attention the prologue of the Gospel of St. John.
3 To tell to the children a story from the Bible.

# THE GOOD EARTH

# Thursday of Sexagesima

### God speaks to us

*Other seed fell upon good ground, and sprang up and yielded fruit a hundred-fold.*
—Gospel of Sunday: St. Luke 8:8

### Meditation

If God has spoken to us in so many ways, how is it that this divine seed, so rich, so effective, so powerful in itself, bears sometimes so little fruit? Why does the divine word not transform more entirely the hearts of men and our own heart? Our Lord teaches us why in the parable of the sower.

For seed to produce fruit, it is not enough that it be healthy, or good, or rich in itself. It also has to fall upon good earth. And Our Lord tells us that in just the same way, for the divine word—which is all powerful, which is holy in itself—to produce fruit, our soul has to be disposed to receive it.

Indeed, the word of God, which in itself is very fruitful, does not always bear its fruits because of the obstacles that we place before it. The devil, our own cares, the constant noise of the media, the wealth and pleasures of life, are as many obstacles which hinder the word of God from bearing within us lasting fruits of holiness.

Let us be clear-sighted about the extent of the combat, that we may be valiant in adversity and not grow discouraged at the first sign of difficulty. To lessen the influence of the devil, let us have recourse to what is stronger than he. Let us have recourse to our guardian angel, let us have recourse to prayer and the sacraments. And let us not lose confidence: God is more powerful to save us than the devil is to destroy us.

Let us also learn to see our cares in perspective by living in the present moment under the eyes of God; let us restrain our disordered appetite of curiosity; and let us be detached from earthly goods and passing pleasures.

In order to preserve our peace of soul and stay masters of ourselves, let us not hesitate to take time for God and let us live in a spirit of abandonment to divine providence, all in developing our talents. Let us follow the advice of the Psalmist, telling us, "Cast thy care upon the Lord, and He shall sustain thee" (Ps. 54:23).

In this way will our soul become good ground.

## Prayer

Lord, behold me here before Thee. Turn my heart into good ground, ready to welcome Thy divine word and to let it bear fruit.
—Fr. Gabriel, DI, II, p. 30

*Or:*

O God, who hast created this earth, who hast enriched it with divine seed, watered it with the blood of Thy Son, give also the grace that it be fruitful, for its salvation and for Thy glory.
—Fr. Emmanuel, M, p. 95

## Thoughts

- We have to render, if we are able, more than we have received, as do the fertile fields that yield incomparably more seed than had been sown within them.
—St. Francis de Sales, TD, September 7

- Just as the earth cannot produce anything if the sun does not make it fruitful, so also we cannot do any good without the grace of God.
—Curé of Ars, TD1, February 4

## Resolutions

1 To make 10 minutes of silent meditation in the morning in order to live closer to God and to draw down His grace upon us.

2 To recite the prayer to St. Michael the Archangel (see end of booklet).

3 To fight against sterile anxieties by abandoning ourselves to God.

# RECEPTIVITY TO THE WORD OF GOD

# Friday of Sexagesima

### GOD SPEAKS TO US

*That seed fallen upon good ground, these are they who, with a right and good heart, having heard the word, hold it fast, and bear fruit in patience.*
—Gospel of Sunday: St. Luke 8:15

### MEDITATION

Let us try today to make an examination of conscience as to the way in which we receive the word of God.

How do I react before the word of God? Am I receptive to the divine word? Am I that good earth which produces fruit a hundred-fold? Or do I not have a tendency to sift the truths of the Faith through my reason and only retain those which please me?

One of the classic defects of man today, in postmodern Western society, consists in wanting to understand everything and in refusing systematically whatever does not fit into his little mind; and that because man looks too much at himself and forgets to consider his nothingness before the infinite majesty of God.

Consequently, we have to be convinced that God knows Himself and that He knows us better than we know ourselves. It is therefore with the greatest respect, with the greatest reverence, with the greatest submission that we ought to welcome the truths of the Faith.

Let us remember that the motive of our Faith is not the evidence of the truths which are taught to us, but rather the authority of God who reveals them. God cannot be deceived nor can He deceive me. If therefore He tells me that there is a Heaven and a Hell and that they are eternal, I ought to believe it. If He tells me that someone committing a single mortal sin deserves that Hell, I ought to believe it. If He tells me that prayer and the sacraments are the most effective weapons to fight against my evil tendencies, I ought to believe it. And so on through all the other truths.

Since God has made Himself known to us through Revelation, let us therefore ask for the grace of an ever deeper faith in revealed truths. Let us know how to preserve preciously all of the messages of God so that they might be within us a source of life.

Let us ask for that grace through the intercession of the most Blessed Virgin, she who is at once the perfect model of the contemplative soul and of docility to the will of God. Let us be as receptive as Our Lady to hear the word of God and above all as generous to say after her from the depths of our heart, *Fiat mihi secundum verbum tuum*, "Be it done to me according to thy word" (Lk. 1:38).

## Prayer

O Eternal Word, Word of my God, I want to spend my life in listening to Thee, to become wholly teachable that I may learn all from Thee.
—Elizabeth of the Trinity, *Prayer to the Trinity*

*Or:*

Come therefore, Word of God, Eternal Word, divine seed, celestial grain of wheat, come into us, come to die there, come to live there and to live eternally.
—Fr. Emmanuel, M, p. 94

## Thoughts

- Blessed the ears of the soul alert enough, recollected enough to hear this voice of the Word of God.
  —Elizabeth of the Trinity, *Heaven in Faith*[48]

- We must listen with faithful attention to the sacred words of God which come from the mouth of those in whom He has placed them, and, as we listen to them, we must often raise our mind to God to ask Him for the grace to benefit from them.
  —St. Vincent de Paul, TD2, March 24

---

[48] *The Complete Works, Vol. 1: I Have Found God*, ICS Publications, 1984, p. 99.

## Resolutions

1. To reread the Gospel from Sunday.
2. To make an examination of conscience on my manner of receiving the word of God.
3. To remember an idea from the sermon last Sunday or from another sermon which especially struck me.

# THE GOOD FRUITS

# Saturday of Sexagesima

### God speaks to us

*In this is My Father glorified, that you bear very much fruit.*

—St. John 15:8

### Meditation

The seed which falls into the good ground produces good fruits. Thus, the faithful Catholic not only saves his own soul, but he does good to those around him. All in detesting error, he looks with compassion on souls who have gone astray and he desires their conversion. His Catholic heart attracts souls of good will and helps them to find the path of salvation.

Jesus detested error, but He loved sinners. Meek and humble of heart, He attracted souls by His goodness. On the contrary, the Pharisees, whose heart was filled with pride, did not know how to recognize Jesus or how to convert souls. Jesus loved merciful hearts and also upright hearts. An upright heart is the contrary of a double heart. This uprightness of heart is essentially an interior disposition of the soul, but it can also be seen externally.

That is why, if we want to have the influence which Jesus desires from us, we have to be 100% Catholic. St. Thomas Aquinas affirms that our external behavior is an object of virtue because it is the indication of interior dispositions.[49] The body is the mirror of the soul. It is written in the Old Testament, "The attire of the body, and the laughter of the teeth, and the gait of the man, show what he is" (Ecclus. 19:27). St. Ambrose likewise said that, "the outward man reveals the hidden man of our heart: frivolous, boastful, or boisterous, or, on the other hand, steady, firm, pure,

---

[49] *Summa Theologica*, IIaIIae, q. 168, a. 1.

and dependable."[50] So others judge us by the outside, and there we have a magnificent field of apostolate.

Therefore let us manifest by our bearing that Jesus reigns in us. Let us spread a sweet fragrance among souls by the perfume of our virtues. Let us draw them by the Holy Trinity who dwells in us. May contact with us give them the desire to be better. We can then be that good seed which yields fruit a hundred-fold, for the glory of God and the salvation of souls.

## Prayer

I abandon and hand over all my being, for time and eternity, to Thy mercy, begging Thee in all the humility of my heart to accomplish in me Thine eternal designs, and not to allow me to offer them any obstacle.
—St. Jane de Chantal, R, p. 11

*Or:*

My God, I adore Thee: Ah, Lord, I give Thee my heart; grant that I many never offend Thee, but that I may do Thy will in all things.
—St. Vincent de Paul, TD2, July 4

## Thoughts

- The word of God always has a strong vital force, capable of bearing not only a certain fruit of Christian living, but abundant fruits of sanctity.
  —Fr. Gabriel, DI, II, p. 30

- Remember to examine your heart often, whether it stands toward your neighbor as you would like his to stand toward you, were you in his place.
  —St. Francis de Sales, TD, April 22

---

[50] *On the Duties of the Clergy*, bk. I, ch. 18. *Cf. Nicene and Post-Nicene Fathers*, Second Series, Vol. 10, Christian Literature Publishing Co., 1896.

## Resolutions

1. To recite very slowly the *Our Father*, with astonishment and wonder, as if we had just discovered that prayer.
2. To act with purity of intention, without turning in on ourselves.
3. To bear witness to our faith with gentleness and in a manner that is convincing.

# THE FORETELLING OF THE PASSION

# Sunday of Quinquagesima

## God speaks to us

*The Son of Man will be delivered to the Gentiles, and will be mocked and scourged and spit upon; and after they have scourged Him, they will put Him to death.*

—Gospel: St. Luke 18:32-33

## Meditation

Taking as a given our desire to follow Jesus and to correspond with His grace, the Church reminds us today of the divine plan of Redemption by the prediction of the Passion of Our Lord. And so she prepares us gradually for Lent, which is going to bring us to Passiontide, when we will live again those heart-rending hours of the sufferings and the death of Our Lord on the Cross.

Three times did Jesus foretell His Passion to the apostles. It was the third prophecy which is recounted in the Gospel today: "Behold, we are going up to Jerusalem, and all things that have been written concerning the Son of Man will be accomplished. *For He will be delivered to the Gentiles, and will be mocked and scourged and spit upon; and after they have scourged Him, they will put Him to death*; and on the third day He will rise again." (Lk. 18:31-33) What is obscure in these words? The language is simple and clear. It does not have some double interpretation. The prediction itself is luminous; it is not veiled under images or parables. And yet, as on the previous occasions, the disciples "understood none of these things and this saying was hidden from them" (Lk. 8:34).

The Church presents to us this passage on the threshold of Lent so as to prepare us to contemplate in our turn this mystery which she will bring to life before us by her liturgy in Passiontide, but also to place us on our guard against the same stumbling block that the apostles encountered.

We are not sheltered from temptation any more than they were; we are not sheltered from a fall like that of Peter during the Passion.

And it is to prevent such a misunderstanding and such an act of frailty, that the Church foretells to us clearly today the Passion of Our Lord and unveils for us the human reaction of the apostles before this prophecy of Jesus Christ.

Let us therefore learn to trust Our Lord and to submit ourselves to the plan of God. It is the most sure means for keeping our peace on this earth and for reaching one day the eternal blessedness of Heaven.

## Prayer

O Jesus! You love men with a truly passionate heart, and many have only disdain and indifference for Thy sacrament of love. I desire, in the measure of my strength, to console Thee for so much ingratitude.

—St. Alphonsus Liguori

*Or:*

Passion of Christ, strengthen me. O good Jesus, hear me. Never allow me to be separated from Thee. From the malicious enemy, defend me. In the hour of my death, call me, and bid me come to Thee, that with Thy saints I may praise Thee, for ever and ever.

—Prayer *Soul of Christ*

## Thoughts

- The human eye does not have the light necessary for understanding the value of the Cross; it takes a new light, the light of the Holy Ghost.

  —Fr. Gabriel, DI, II, p. 57

- Jesus loved me—that is the only word that explains the Cross; it is the great lesson that Jesus crucified teaches to us. Let us embrace the Cross, and even more Him who is nailed there for us.

  —Fr. Emmanuel, M, p. 142

## RESOLUTIONS

1. To read with attention the proper texts of the Mass.
2. To meditate for 10 minutes on the Passion of Jesus.
3. To prepare our Lenten resolutions.

# THE INCOMPREHENSION OF THE APOSTLES

# Monday of Quinquagesima

### God speaks to us

*O foolish ones and slow of heart to believe in all that the prophets have spoken! Did not the Christ have to suffer these things before entering into His glory?*

—St. Luke 24:25-26

### Meditation

What is the reason for this incomprehension of the apostles before so clear a prophecy of the Passion of Jesus? They love Our Lord and they cannot reconcile themselves to the idea that He will have to suffer. Moreover, "He had called them to follow Him and accompany Him, and they had no doubt that they would also have to share in all of His states of life."[51] They therefore realize that, if their divine Master has to pass through suffering, they themselves will have to pass through it, also. They do not want to accept this, and neither do we.

That is why it is good for us today to ask Jesus for the understanding of this mystery of the Cross, and more precisely the understanding of the mystery of our own Cross as a source of sanctification.

Man has a selective ear. When a person informs him of some event which bothers him, which upsets his manner of thinking or his manner of acting, he has a tendency to close himself inwardly. This explains the apostles' difficulty in understanding the Passion of Our Lord; it explains our own difficulty in accepting the mystery of the Cross in our life or in the life of the Church.

So man understands the truths that go in the sense of his natural inclinations, but he has a hard time admitting the truths that are contrary to his desires. That God is merciful, yes, that is a truth that suits me; I

---

[51] Bossuet, *Oratorical Works*, V, pp. 240-241.

have no difficulty admitting it. But that Hell is eternal, now that is already more difficult to picture.

And for the Passion of Our Lord, it is the same thing. It seems perfectly natural that Jesus should triumph over His enemies. But that He should let Himself be captured and martyred by them, is something that we have a harder time understanding.

Yes, let us admit it: still today, the Cross is repugnant to our sensibility and even to our will; or at least, if we manage to love the Cross in the abstract, we have a harder time loving our own personal Cross. And so let us ask Our Lord for the grace to adore the mystery of the Cross, to accept it in our everyday life, that we might come one day to the glory of the resurrection.

## Prayer

O Jesus, give me the light to understand the mystery and the value of Christian suffering.

—Fr. Gabriel, DI, II, p. 56

*Or:*

O Lord, grant me to recognize and embrace Thy Cross in every suffering, physical or moral, so that I might associate myself intimately with Thy Passion for the salvation of souls.

—Fr. Gabriel, DI, II, p. 66

## Thoughts

- If the apostles do not hear the very obvious words of the Savior Jesus, it is because not only their mind, but also their will is ill disposed... A preoccupied mind cannot receive the light; a depraved will avoids and fears it.

  —Bossuet, OW, V, p. 229

- Suffering has a supernatural value only when we suffer with Christ and for Him. It is Jesus who sanctifies pain; far from Him, it is worthless and has no purpose.

  —Fr. Gabriel, DI, II, p. 65

## Resolutions

1 To recite one of the sorrowful mysteries of the rosary.
2 To accept the vexations of the day in a spirit of faith.
3 To practice the virtue of patience in our family and at work.

# CONFIDENT RESIGNATION

# Tuesday of Quinquagesima

## God speaks to us

*God forbid that I should glory save in the Cross of Our Lord Jesus Christ, through whom the world is crucified to me, and I to the world.*
—Epistle of St. Paul to the Galatians 6:14

## Meditation

Our holy religion teaches us not only to adore the abasements and humiliations of Our Lord, but to adore likewise the sufferings and the humiliations which God sends to us to work our salvation.

Indeed, it is not for us to determine the size of our cross. God knows better than we do what is suitable for us, and that is why it does not belong to us to choose our cross or to measure it, but only to carry it with submission and patience, keeping a gaze of love on Jesus crucified.

The Passion of Our Lord teaches us that God allows suffering as a means of expressing our love. Suffering is the sacrificial matter of love. The degree of our love is measured by the degree of suffering which we are capable of enduring for the one beloved.

The sufferings of Our Lord also teach us to mortify the concupiscence of the eyes and of the flesh, as well as the pride of life. Naturally, man seeks for honors, man seeks his own comfort; he desires wealth. That is why suffering is so repugnant to his fallen nature.

The Cross of Our Lord teaches us that humiliations and poverty are necessary. That is why we instinctively reject it. The same thing explains the reaction of the apostles, which we saw in last Sunday's Gospel. They refuse the suffering Messiah because they know that they are called to follow Him, to imitate Him, for He is their Master and their model. If Our Lord is to suffer, they too will suffer, and it is what they cannot bring themselves to accept.

Yet, suffering well accepted is a powerful remedy to correct the disordered love which we have of ourselves, that disordered attachment which we have for the goods of this world and for the pleasures of the present life.

And so, let us ask today Our Lady of Sorrows to help us to carry generously our cross, in the footsteps of her divine Son.

## Prayer

O Lord, I beg of Thee, help me to free myself from the slavery of the body! Teach me to dominate its excessive demands, to mortify its claims.

—Fr. Gabriel, DI, II, p. 62

*Or:*

O my Jesus! The Cross is Thy standard; I would be ashamed to pray that Thou wouldst deliver me from it.

—Fr. Gabriel, DI, II, p. 59

## Thoughts

- Our passions, our innate tendency to enjoy, often cry out in us and try by a thousand pretexts to hinder us from following Jesus crucified. Let us remain firm in our faith.

  —Fr. Gabriel, DI, II, p. 58

- Each one of us, in the trials that are sent to him, in the sacrifices which are held out to him, ought to understand this one thing: that the cross is a visit from love.

  —Fr. Calmel, TD, April 6

## Resolutions

1. To accept humiliations in a spirit of reparation for our sins.
2. To meditate for five minutes on one station of the Way of the Cross.
3. To offer to God the sufferings of our illness or of any other painful vexation: a humiliation, a loss of money, a failure.

# THE PRESENTATION OF JESUS IN THE TEMPLE

# February 2nd

## God speaks to us

*When the days of Mary's purification were fulfilled according to the Law of Moses, they took Him up to Jerusalem to present Him to the Lord.*
—Gospel: St. Luke 2:22

## Meditation

Slaves of the Egyptians, the Hebrews begged for a liberator, and God raised up Moses to lead them into the promised land. But it took the 10 plagues of Egypt, the last of which was the death of the firstborn of the Egyptians, to win the consent of Pharaoh. While the firstborn of the Hebrews were protected thanks to the blood of the lamb smeared on the lintel of the doors of their houses, the firstborn of the Egyptians were exterminated by the angel of God. From then onward, in thanksgiving for that special protection by God, the Hebrews made the offering of their eldest son, as it is written in the book of Numbers: "God spoke to Moses in these words: On the day when I struck all of the firstborn of the land of Egypt, I consecrated to myself every firstborn in Israel" (*Cf.* Ex. 13:1-2 and 15).

It is therefore in a spirit of obedience and gratitude that Our Lady submits herself today to this law. Oh, certainly! She had not waited for this day to make the interior offering of her Son to God. She had already offered Jesus from the very day of His conception in her womb. But today she expresses the interior state of her soul in a visible way.

In a tremendous act of magnanimity, she offers Our Lord to His Father. She offers Him not only as an individual, as an isolated person, but as the future head of the mystical body which is the Church. Consequently, we are already present in that offering. Yes, it is no exaggeration to think that in offering her divine Son for the salvation of the world,

Our Lady is already thinking of all of the souls that will benefit by the fruits of the Passion.

In making this offering with such a beautiful state of soul, she responds perfectly to God's expectations. Today, as on the day of the Annunciation, she says again her *Fiat*: "Be it done unto me according to thy word" (Lk. 1:38), I offer Thee my divine Son and I accept already all the consequences of this offering. Then does the old man Simeon foretell that her Son will be "a sign of contradiction" (Lk. 2:34); as for herself, "[her] own soul a sword shall pierce" (Lk. 2:35).

## Prayer

Purify my soul, O Lord, so that it might be totally penetrated by Thy light and Thy love.

—Fr. Gabriel, DI, p. 6

*Or:*

O obedient Virgin! May your prompt obedience serve as forgiveness for our rebellion; may all burdens be light for us, in obeying after your holy example.

—St. Jeanne de France, R, p. 11

## Thoughts

- Let us unite ourselves therefore to the Blessed Virgin offering her Son, and let us offer with her this blessed Child, this elect of God, in whom God is well pleased. Let us offer Him for our sins; let us offer Him as the divine Lamb who bears the sins of the world; as the veritable Son of God, who alone is pleasing to His eyes.

  —Fr. Chevrier, R, p. 11

- Oh! How happy are those souls that are all given to God and who in truth may say: Jesus is all that I have and I am all His.

  —St. Jane de Chantal, R, p. 11

## Resolutions

1 To recite the fourth joyful mystery of the rosary.

2 To read in our missal and meditate for a few minutes on the prayers of the blessing of the candles.

3 To respond to the love of Jesus and Mary by a prompt and joyful obedience.

# Prayers

# Spiritual Communion

A spiritual communion consists in an ardent desire to receive Jesus in the Blessed Sacrament, as well as an act of love such as one would make if one had received Him sacramentally.[1] The Council of Trent strongly praises spiritual communion and encourages the faithful to practice it.[2]

To make a good spiritual communion, St. Alphonsus Liguori recommends the following act:

> My Jesus, I believe that Thou art present in the Most Blessed Sacrament. I love Thee above all things, and I desire to receive Thee into my soul. Since I cannot now receive Thee sacramentally, come at least spiritually into my heart. I embrace Thee as if Thou wert already come, and unite myself wholly to Thee. Never permit me to be separated from Thee. Amen.

Depending on the circumstances, if one needs a shorter prayer or if one prefers a more rapid form, the same saint proposes that we very simply say:

> O Jesus, I believe that Thou art in the Most Blessed Sacrament! Come into my heart. I embrace Thee; oh, never leave me![3]

---

[1] St. Thomas Aquinas, *Summa Theologica*, IIIa, q. 80, a. 1, *ad* 3.
[2] Council of Trent, Session XIII, Decree Concerning the Sacrament of the Eucharist, Ch. 8.
[3] St. Alphonsus Liguori, *Visits to the Blessed Sacrament and the Blessed Virgin Mary*, TAN, 2001, p. 14-15.

# The Mysteries of the Rosary

## Joyful Mysteries

First mystery: The Annunciation of the Angel Gabriel to the Virgin Mary; fruit of this mystery: humility

Second mystery: The Visitation of Our Lady to her cousin Elizabeth; fruit of this mystery: fraternal charity

Third mystery: The birth of Jesus in the stable at Bethlehem; fruit of this mystery: the spirit of poverty

Fourth mystery: The Presentation of the child Jesus in the Temple; fruit of this mystery: obedience

Fifth mystery: The finding of the child Jesus in the Temple; fruit of this mystery: the seeking of God in all things.

## Sorrowful Mysteries

First mystery: The agony of Jesus in the Garden of Olives; fruit of this mystery: contrition for our sins

Second mystery: The scourging of Our Lord at the pillar; fruit of this mystery: the mortification of the senses

Third mystery: The crowning with thorns; fruit of this mystery: the mortification of pride

Fourth mystery: The carrying of the Cross; fruit of this mystery: patience and perseverance in trials

Fifth mystery: The crucifixion and death of Jesus on the Cross; fruit of this mystery: a greater love of God and of souls.

## Glorious Mysteries

First mystery: The Resurrection of Our Lord; fruit of this mystery: faith

Second mystery: The Ascension of Jesus into Heaven; fruit of this mystery: hope

Third mystery: The descent of the Holy Ghost on the Blessed Virgin and the apostles; fruit of this mystery: missionary zeal

Fourth mystery: The Assumption of Our Lady into Heaven; fruit of this mystery: the grace of a happy death

Fifth mystery: The crowning of Mary as queen of Heaven and earth; fruit of this mystery: a great devotion to the Blessed Virgin.

# Act of Faith

O my God, I firmly believe that Thou art one God in three divine Persons, the Father, the Son, and the Holy Ghost; I believe that Thy divine Son became man and died for our sins, and that He will come to judge the living and the dead. I believe these and all the truths which the holy Catholic Church teaches, because Thou hast revealed them, who canst neither deceive nor be deceived.

# Act of Hope

O my God, relying on Thy infinite goodness and promises, I hope to obtain pardon of my sins, the help of Thy grace, and life everlasting, through the merits of Jesus Christ, my Lord and Redeemer.

# Act of Charity

O my God, I love Thee above all things, with my whole heart and soul, because Thou art all good and worthy of all my love. I love my neighbor as myself for love of Thee. I forgive all who have injured me and ask pardon of all whom I have injured.

# Act of Contrition

O my God, I am heartily sorry for having offended Thee, and I detest all my sins because I dread the loss of Heaven and the pains of Hell, but most of all because they offend Thee, my God, who art all good and deserving of all my love. I firmly resolve, with the help of Thy grace, to confess my sins, to do penance, and to amend my life.

# Prayer of the Angel at Fatima

My God, I believe, I adore, I hope, and I love Thee; I beg pardon for those who do not believe, do not adore, do not hope, and do not love Thee.

# Prayer to the Holy Ghost

Come, Holy Ghost, fill the hearts of Thy faithful, and enkindle in them the fire of Thy love.
V. Send forth Thy Spirit, and they shall be created.
R. And Thou shalt renew the face of the earth.
Let us pray: O God, who by the light of the Holy Ghost didst instruct the hearts of the faithful, grant us by the same Spirit to be truly wise and ever to rejoice in His consolation. Through the same Christ Our Lord. Amen.

# *Memorare* of St. Bernard

## (1090-1153)

Remember, O most gracious Virgin Mary, that never was it known that anyone who fled to thy protection, implored thy help or sought thy intercession was left unaided. Inspired by this confidence, I fly unto thee, O Virgin of virgins, my Mother; to thee do I come, before thee I stand, sinful and sorrowful.

O Mother of the Word Incarnate, despise not my petitions, but in thy clemency hear and answer me. Amen.

# Prayer to St. Michael the Archangel

St. Michael the Archangel, defend us in battle, be our protection against the wickedness and the snares of the devil. May God rebuke Him, we humbly pray, and do thou, O Prince of the heavenly host, by the power of God, cast into Hell Satan and all the evil spirits who wander throughout the world seeking the ruin of souls. Amen.

# Prayer to St. Joseph

## Patron of the Universal Church

To thee, O blessed Joseph, do we have recourse in our tribulation, and, having implored the help of thy thrice-holy Spouse, we confidently invoke thy patronage also. By that charity wherewith thou wast united to the immaculate Virgin Mother of God, and by that fatherly affection with which thou didst embrace the Child Jesus, we beseech thee and we humbly pray, that thou wouldst look graciously upon the inheritance which Jesus Christ hath purchased by His Blood, and assist us in our needs by thy power and strength.

Most watchful guardian of the Holy Family, protect the chosen people of Jesus Christ; keep far from us, most loving father, all blight of error and corruption: mercifully assist us from Heaven, most mighty defender, in this our conflict with the powers of darkness; and, even as of old thou didst rescue the Child Jesus from the supreme peril of His life, so now defend God's Holy Church from the snares of the enemy and from all adversity; keep us one and all under thy continual protection, that we may be supported by thine example and thine assistance, may be enabled to lead a holy life, die a happy death and come at last to the possession of everlasting blessedness in Heaven. Amen.

# Prayer of St. Pius X

## To the Glorious St. Joseph, Model of Workers

Glorious St. Joseph, pattern of all who are devoted to toil, obtain for me the grace to toil in the spirit of penance, in order thereby to atone for my many sins; to toil conscientiously, putting devotion to duty before my own inclinations; to labor with thankfulness and joy, deeming it an honor to employ and to develop, by my labor, the gifts I have received from Almighty God; to work with order, peace, moderation, and patience, without ever shrinking from weariness and difficulties; to work above all with a pure intention and with detachment from self, having always before my eyes the hour of death and the accounting which I must then render of time ill-spent, of talents unemployed, of good undone, and of my empty pride in success, which is so fatal to the work of God. All for Jesus, all through Mary, all in imitation of thee, O Patriarch Joseph! This shall be my motto in life and in death. Amen.

# Act of Confidence in God

## St. Claude de la Colombière

My God, I am firmly convinced that Thou keepest watch over those who hope in Thee, and that we can want for nothing when we look for all from Thee, that I am resolved in the future to live free from every care, and to turn all my anxieties over to Thee. "In the peace I find in Thee I will sleep, and I will rest: for Thou, O Lord, hast singularly settled me in the hope I have of Thy divine goodness" (Ps. 4:9-10). Men may deprive me of possessions and of honor; sickness may strip me of strength and the means of serving Thee; I may even lose Thy grace by sin; but I shall never lose my hope. I shall keep it until the last moment of my life; and at that moment all the demons in Hell shall strive to tear it from me in vain. "In the peace I find in Thee I will sleep and I will rest..." Others may look for happiness from their wealth or their talents; others may rest on the innocence of their life, or the severity of their penance, or the amount of their alms, or the fervor of their prayers; "for Thou, O Lord, hast singularly settled me in hope." As for me, Lord, all my confidence is my confidence itself. This confidence has never deceived anyone. No one, no one has hoped in Thee, Lord, and has been confounded (Ecclus. 2:11).

I am sure, therefore, that I shall be eternally happy, since I firmly hope to be, and because it is from Thee, O God, that I hope for it. "In Thee, O Lord, have I hoped, let me never be confounded" (Ps. 30:2). I know, alas, I know only too well, that I am weak and unstable. I know what temptation can do against the strongest virtue. I have seen the stars of heaven fall, and the pillars of the firmament; but that cannot frighten me. So long as I continue to hope, I shall be sheltered from all misfortune; and I am sure of hoping always, since I hope also for this unwavering hopefulness.

Finally, I am sure that I cannot hope too much in Thee, and that I cannot receive less than I have hoped for from Thee. So

## Act of Confidence in God

I hope that Thou wilt hold me safe on the steepest slopes, that Thou wilt sustain me against the most furious assaults, and that Thou wilt make my weakness triumph over my most fearful enemies. I hope that Thou wilt love me always, and that I too shall love Thee without ceasing. To carry my hope once and for all as far as it can go, I hope from Thee to possess Thee, O my Creator, in time and in eternity. Amen.

# Prayer to the Curé of Ars for Vocations

O blessed John Mary Vianney, whom the almighty and merciful God made wondrous by your pastoral zeal and your constant love of prayer and penance, obtain for the clergy, by your intercession, that same zeal and those same virtues.

Ask for us, you whose heart was adorned by angelic purity, that our priests may preserve the character of their ordination pure and without stain. May they, after your example, be firm in the Catholic Faith, intrepid in spreading the kingdom of their divine Master, never failing evangelists of revealed truth.

In imitation of your own heart, may their heart detach itself from creatures and from goods that pass away.

Incomparable worker in the field entrusted to your labor, obtain the realization of Jesus' wish. The harvest is abundant, the workers are few. Pray the Master of the harvest to send us good workers.

O blessed Vianney, intercede for the clergy. May your patronage and your prayer obtain an abundance of genuine priestly vocations. May the Holy Spirit raise up imitators of you. May He give us saints. Amen.

# A Prayer for Priests

My God,
I pray to Thee for Thy priests,
For all Thy priests.
I ask of Thee to make them saints;
I ask of Thee that they might love profoundly their sacrifice
And might live it with love.
I ask of Thee to grant them obedience,
A spirit of detachment,
A chastity as strong as it is crystal-clear.
And also abnegation, humility,
Kindness, zeal, fidelity.
I ask of Thee that no soul might draw near to them
Without loving Thee more.
I ask of Thee, my God,
That through them Thou might sow Marian graces
Throughout the world,
Revealing to what extent
Mary is our Mother.
And that it might be so,
That Thy Reign might spread
And be strengthened, by them, over all the earth,
I promise you, O Jesus, to immolate myself
By Thy side,
With all my heart.
Amen.

# Litany of Humility[4]

O Jesus, meek and humble of heart, *hear me.*
From the desire of being esteemed, *deliver me, Jesus.*
From the desire of being loved,
From the desire of being extolled,
From the desire of being honored,
From the desire of being praised,
From the desire of being preferred to others,
From the desire of being consulted,
From the desire of being approved,
From the fear of being humiliated,
From the fear of being despised,
From the fear of suffering rebukes,
From the fear of being calumniated,
From the fear of being forgotten,
From the fear of being ridiculed,
From the fear of being wronged,
From the fear of being suspected,

That others may be loved more than I, *Jesus, grant me the grace to desire it.*

That others may be esteemed more than I,

That, in the opinion of the world, others may increase and I may decrease,

That others may be chosen and I set aside,

That others may be praised and I go unnoticed,

That others may be preferred to me in everything,

That others may become holier than I, provided that I may become as holy as I should, *Jesus, grant me the grace to desire it.*

---

[4] Composed by Cardinal Merry del Val and discovered after his death.

# Litany of the Precious Blood

Lord, have mercy on us. *Lord, have mercy on us.*
Christ, have mercy on us. *Christ, have mercy on us.*
Lord, have mercy on us. *Lord, have mercy on us.*
Christ, hear us. *Christ, hear us.*
Christ, graciously hear us. *Christ, graciously hear us.*
God the Father of Heaven, *have mercy on us.*
God the Son, Redeemer of the world,
God, the Holy Ghost,
Holy Trinity, One God,
Blood of Christ, only-begotten Son of the eternal Father, *save us.*
Blood of Christ, Incarnate Word of God,
Blood of Christ, of the New and Eternal Testament,
Blood of Christ, falling upon the earth in the Agony,
Blood of Christ, shed profusely in the Scourging,
Blood of Christ, flowing forth in the Crowning with Thorns,
Blood of Christ, poured out on the Cross,
Blood of Christ, price of our salvation,
Blood of Christ, without which there is no forgiveness,
Blood of Christ, eucharistic drink and refreshment of souls,
Blood of Christ, stream of mercy,
Blood of Christ, victor over demons,
Blood of Christ, courage of Martyrs,
Blood of Christ, strength of Confessors,
Blood of Christ, bringing forth Virgins,
Blood of Christ, help of those in peril,
Blood of Christ, relief of the burdened,
Blood of Christ, solace in sorrow,
Blood of Christ, hope of the penitent,
Blood of Christ, consolation of the dying,
Blood of Christ, peace and tenderness of hearts,
Blood of Christ, pledge of eternal life,
Blood of Christ, freeing souls from Purgatory,
Blood of Christ, most worthy of all glory and honor,

Lamb of God, who taketh away the sins of the world, *spare us, O Lord.*

Lamb of God, who taketh away the sins of the world, *graciously hear us, O Lord.*

Lamb of God, who taketh away the sins of the world, *have mercy on us, O Lord.*

V. Thou hast redeemed us, O Lord, in Thy Blood.

R. And made us, for our God, a kingdom.

Let us pray:

Almighty and eternal God, Thou hast appointed Thine only-begotten Son the Redeemer of the world and willed to be appeased by His blood. Grant, we beg of Thee, that we may worthily adore this price of our salvation and through its power be safeguarded from the evils of the present life so that we may rejoice in its fruits forever in Heaven. Through the same Christ Our Lord. Amen.

# Latin Hymns

## Hymn of Vespers of the Holy Family

*O Lux beata cælitum,*
*Et summa spes mortalium,*
*Jesu, o cui domestica*
*Arrisit orto caritas:*

O blessed light of saints and angels and highest hope of men on earth, O Jesus, whose eyes first opened upon the smile of a loving home;

*Maria, dives gratia,*
*O sola quæ casto potes*
*Fovere Jesum pectore,*
*Cum lacte donans oscula:*

O Mary, rich in grace, who alone may warm Jesus at your pure breast, kissing His tiny hands as you nourish Him with your milk;

*Tuque ex vetustis patribus*
*Delecte custos Virginis,*
*Dulci patris quem nomine*
*Divina Proles invocat:*

And thou, honored among all the patriarchs of old, chosen as guardian of the Virgin, whom the divine Child calls by the sweet name of father;

*De stirpe Jesse nobili*
*Nati in salutem gentium,*
*Audite nos, qui supplices*
*Vestras ad aras sistimus.*

Ye three, born of the noble line of Jesse for the redemption of the nations, hear us, who kneel here in supplication before your holy sanctuary.

*Dum sol redux ad vesperum*
*Rebus nitorem detrahit,*
*Nos hic manentes intimo*
*Ex corde vota fundimus.*

As the sun returns to evening and leaves all things in twilight, we still linger on your threshold, prayers welling up from the depths of our heart.

*Qua vestra sedes floruit*
*Virtutis omnis gratia,*
*Hanc detur in domesticis*
*Referre posse moribus.*

May that grace of all virtue, which transformed thy home into a sweet garden, blossom around our humble hearth, in our own life as a family.

*Jesu, tuis obœdiens*
*Qui factus es parentibus,*
*Cum Patre summo ac Spiritu*
*Semper tibi sit gloria. Amen.*

O Jesus, who were made obedient to Thy parents, glory be to Thee always, equally with the Father and the divine Spirit. Amen.

## Dies Iræ

*Dies iræ, dies illa,*  
*Solvet sæclum in favilla,*  
*teste David cum Sibylla.*

The day of wrath, that awful day, shall reduce the world to ashes, as David and the Sibyl prophesied.

*Quantus tremor est futurus,*  
*Quando Judex est venturus,*  
*cuncta stricte discussurus.*

How great will be the terror, when the Judge shall come to examine all things rigorously!

*Tuba mirum spargens sonum*  
*Per sepulcra regionum,*  
*Coget omnes ante thronum.*

The trumpet, with astounding blast, echoing over the sepulchres of the whole world, shall summon all before the throne.

*Mors stupebit et natura,*  
*Cum resurget creatura,*  
*Judicanti responsura.*

Death and nature will stand aghast, when the creature shall rise again, to answer before his Judge.

*Liber scriptus proferetur,*  
*In quo totum continetur,*  
*Unde mundus judicetur.*

The written book shall be brought forth, containing all for which the world must be judged.

*Judex ergo cum sedebit,*  
*Quidquid latet apparebit:*  
*Nil inultum remanebit.*

When, therefore, the Judge shall be seated, whatsoever is hidden shall be brought to light; nought shall remain unpunished.

*Quid sum miser tunc*  
    *dicturus?*  
*Quem patronum rogaturus,*  
*Cum vix justus sit securus?*

What then shall I, unhappy man, allege? Whom shall I invoke as protector, when even the just shall hardly be secure?

*Rex tremendæ majestatis,*  
*Qui salvandos salvas gratis,*  
*Salva me, fons pietatis.*

O King of awful majesty, who of Thy free gift savest them that are to be saved, save me, O fount of mercy!

*Recordare Jesu pie,*  
*Quod sum causa tuæ viæ:*  
*Ne me perdas illa die.*

Remember, O loving Jesus, 'twas for my sake Thou camest on earth: let me not, then, be lost on that day.

| | |
|---|---|
| *Quærens me, sedisti lassus:*<br>*Redemisti crucem passus:*<br>*Tantus labor non sit cassus.* | Seeking me Thou satest weary; Thou redeemedst me by dying on the Cross: let not such suffering be all in vain. |
| *Juste judex ultionis,*<br>*Donum fac remissionis,*<br>*Ante diem rationis.* | O righteous awarder of punishment, grant me the gift of pardon before the reckoning-day. |
| *Ingemisco, tamquam reus:*<br>*Culpa rubet vultus meus:*<br>*Supplicanti parce Deus.* | I groan as one guilty, while I blush for my sins: Oh! Spare Thy suppliant, my God! |
| *Qui Mariam absolvisti,*<br>*Et latronem exaudisti,*<br>*Mihi quoque spem dedisti.* | Thou didst absolve Mary Magdalen, and didst hear the prayer of the thief: to me, then, Thou hast also given hope. |
| *Preces meæ non sunt dignæ:*<br>*Sed tu bonus fac benigne,*<br>*Ne perenni cremer igne.* | My prayers deserve not to be heard; but Thou art good: grant, in Thy kindness, that I may not burn in the unquenchable fire. |
| *Inter oves locum præsta,*<br>*Et ab hædis me sequestra,*<br>*Statuens in parte dextera.* | Give me a place among Thy sheep, separating me from the goats and setting me on Thy right hand. |
| *Confutatis maledictis,*<br>*Flammis acribus addictis.*<br>*Voca me cum benedictis.* | When the reprobate, covered with confusion, shall have been sentenced to the cruel flames, call me with the blessed. |
| *Oro supplex et acclinis,*<br>*Cor contritum quasi cinis:*<br>*Gere curam mei finis.* | Prostrate in supplication I implore Thee, with a heart contrite as though crushed to ashes: Oh! Have care of my last hour! |
| *Lacrimosa dies illa,*<br>*Qua resurget ex favilla.*<br>*Judicandus homo reus:*<br>*Huic ergo parce Deus.* | A mournful day that day shall be, when from the dust shall arise guilty man, that he may be judged; spare him, then, O God! |
| *Pie Jesu Domine,*<br>*Dona eis requiem. Amen.* | O tender Lord Jesus, give them eternal rest. Amen. |

## Magnificat

1. *Magnificat * anima mea Dominum.*

   My soul doth magnify the Lord:

2. *Et exsultavit spiritus meus * in Deo salutari meo.*

   And my spirit hath rejoiced in God my Savior.

3. *Quia respexit humilitatem ancillæ suæ: * ecce enim ex hoc beatam me dicent omnes generationes.*

   Because He hath regarded the humility of His handmaid; for behold from henceforth all generations shall call me blessed.

4. *Quia fecit mihi magna qui potens est: * et sanctum nomen eius.*

   For He that is mighty hath done great things to me: and holy is His name.

5. *Et misericordia eius a progenie in progenies * timentibus eum.*

   And His mercy is from generation to generations, to them that fear Him.

6. *Fecit potentiam in brachio suo: * dispersit superbos mente cordis sui.*

   He hath shown might in His arm: He hath scattered the proud in the conceit of their heart:

7. *Deposuit potentes de sede, * et exaltavit humiles.*

   He hath put down the mighty from their seat, and hath exalted the humble.

8. *Esurientes implevit bonis: * et divites dimisit inanes.*

   He hath filled the hungry with good things: and the rich He hath sent away empty.

9. *Suscepit Israël puerum suum, * recordatus misericordiæ suæ.*

   He hath received Israel His servant, being mindful of His mercy.

10. *Sicut locutus est ad patres nostros, * Abraham et semini eius in sæcula.*

    As He spoke to our fathers, to Abraham and to his seed forever.

11. *Gloria Patri et Filio, * et Spiritui Sancto.*

Glory be to the Father and to the Son and to the Holy Ghost.

12. *Sicut erat in principio, et nunc, et semper, * et in sæcula sæculorum. Amen.*

As it was in the beginning, is now, and ever shall be, world without end. Amen.

# Latin Prayer *Anima Christi*

*Anima Christi, sanctifica me.*
*Corpus Christi, salva me.*
*Sanguis Christi, inebria me.*
*Aqua lateris Christi, lava me.*
*Passio Christi, conforta me.*
*O bone Iesu, exaudi me.*
*Intra tua vulnera, absconde me.*
*Ne permittas me separari a te.*
*Ab hoste maligno, defende me.*
*In hora mortis meæ, voca me,*
*et jube me venire ad te,*
*ut cum Sanctis tuis laudem te,*
*In sæcula sæculorum. Amen.*

# English Prayer *Soul of Christ*

Soul of Christ, sanctify me.
Body of Christ, save me.
Blood of Christ, inebriate me.
Water from the side of Christ, wash me.
Passion of Christ, strengthen me.
O good Jesus, hear me.
In Thy wounds, hide me.
Permit me not to be separated from Thee.
From the malicious enemy, defend me.
At the hour of my death, call me
and bid me come to Thee,
that with Thy saints I may praise Thee,
for ever and ever. Amen.

# Hymn *Soul of My Savior*

Soul of my Savior, sanctify my breast,
Body of Christ, be Thou my saving guest,
Blood of my Savior, bathe me in Thy tide,
Wash me with waters gushing from Thy side.

Strength and protection may Thy Passion be;
O blessèd Jesus, hear and answer me;
Deep in Thy wounds, Lord, hide and shelter me,
So shall I never, never part from Thee.

Guard and defend me from the foe malign,
In death's dread moments make me only Thine;
Call me and bid me come to Thee on high
Where I may praise Thee with Thy saints for aye.

# Bibliography

**Holy Scripture**
    Acts:    Acts of the apostles
    Col.:    Epistle of St. Paul to the Colossians
    Ecclus.:    Ecclesiasticus
    Ex.:    Exodus
    Gal.:    Epistle of St. Paul to the Galatians
    Gen.:    Book of Genesis
    Heb.:    Epistle of St. Paul to the Hebrews
    Jas.:    Epistle of St. James
    Jn.:    Gospel according to St. John
    Lk.:    Gospel according to St. Luke
    Mk.:    Gospel according to St. Mark
    Mt.:    Gospel according to St. Matthew
    Num.:    Numbers
    Ps.:    Psalm
    Prov.:    Proverbs
    Rom.:    Epistle of St. Paul to the Romans
    I Cor.:    First Epistle of St. Paul to the Corinthians
    I Jn.:    First Epistle of St. John

**St. Alphonsus Liguori**

*Holiness Day by Day* [*La sainteté au jour le jour*], Clovis, 2014.

*Visits to the Blessed Sacrament and the Blessed Virgin Mary*, TAN, 2001.

**St. Benedict**

*The Rule of St. Benedict*, Roman Catholic Books, from the translation of Abbot Justin McCann, O.S.B., 1951.

    TD:    *Thought for the Day* [*Une Pensée par jour*], texts selected by Véronique Dupont, O.S.B., Médiaspaul, 2007.

**St. Bernadette**

    W:    *The Writings of St. Bernadette and Her Spiritual Path* [*Les écrits de sainte Bernadette et sa voie spirituelle*], Lethielleux, 1980.

    R:    The Rosary: Texts of St. Bernadette [*Le rosaire, textes de sainte Bernadette*], Monastery of Chambarand.

**Fr. Chevrier**

    R:    *The Rosary: Texts of Fr. Chevrier* [*Le rosaire, textes du père Chevrier*], Monastery of Chambarand.

# Bibliography

**Clement XI**

    Universal Prayer, "Thanksgiving after Mass," in *Diurnale romanum*, 1960.

**Curé of Ars**

  R:   *The Rosary: Texts of the Curé of Ars* [*Le rosaire, textes du saint curé d'Ars*], Monastery of Chambarand.

  ST:   *Selected Thoughts of the Curé of Ars and Little Flowers of Ars* [*Pensée choisies du saint curé d'Ars et petites fleurs d'Ars*], texts selected by Janine Frossard, Téqui, 1961.

  TD1:   *Thought for the Day* [*Une pensée par jour*], Clovis, 2006.

  TD2:   *Thought for the Day*, texts selected by Claudine Fearon, Médiaspaul, 2010.

**Elizabeth of the Trinity**

    *The Complete Works, Vol. 1: I Have Found God*, Institute of Carmelite Studies, 2014.

  L:   *The Complete Works, Vol. 2: Letters from Carmel*, Institute of Carmelite Studies, 2014.

    French Edition: *Œuvres Complètes*, Cerf, 1991.

**Fr. Emmanuel**

  M:   *Meditations for Every Day of the Liturgical Year* [*Méditations pour tous les jours de l'année liturgique*], Dismas, 1987.

**St. Francis de Sales**

  TD:   *Thought for the Day* [*Une pensée par jour*], texts gathered by Sr. Marie-Christophe, Médiaspaul, 2008.

  XXI:   "Letters, XI," in *Works of St. Francis de Sales* [*Œuvres de saint François de Sales*], *XXI*, Librairie Catholique Emmanuel Vitte, 1923.

**St. Gregory the Great**

  TD:   *Thought for the Day* [*Une pensée par jour*], texts selected by Jacqueline Martin-Bagnaudez, Médiaspaul, 2012.

**St. John Chrysostom**

    *Complete Works*, [*Œuvres complètes*], VI, Louis Vivès, 1868.

**St. John of the Cross**

SC: *The Spiritual Canticle*, in *The Collected Works of St. John of the Cross*, Institute of Carmelite Studies, 1991.

**St. Jeanne de Chantal**

R: The Rosary: Texts of St. Jeanne de Chantal [*Le rosaire, textes de sainte Jeanne de Chantal*], monastery of Chambarand.

**St. Jeanne de France**

R: The Rosary: Texts of St. Jeanne de France [*Le rosaire, textes de sainte Jeanne de France*], monastery of Chambarand.

**St. Maximilian Kolbe**

M: Unpublished manuscript.

**Pauline Jaricot**

TD: *Thought for the Day* [*Une pensée par jour*], texts selected by Œuvres Pontificales missionnaires (Lyon), Médiaspaul, 2008.

**Padre Pio**

TD2: *Thought for the Day* [*Une pensée par jour*], texts selected by Fr. Gerardo Di Flumeri, O.F.M. Cap., Médiaspaul, 2010.

**St. Vincent de Paul**

TD1: *Thought for the Day,* [*Une Pensée par jour*], Clovis, 2006.

TD2: *Thought for the Day*, texts gathered by Fr. Jean-Yves Ducourneau, Médiaspaul, 2007.

**Other Authors**

OW: Bossuet, *Oratorical Works* [*Œuvres oratoires*], I and V, Desclée de Brouwer, 1890.

CW: Bourdaloue, *Complete Works* [*Œuvres complètes*], II, L. Guérin, 1864.

Fr. Pierre Caillon, *A Child of Four Has Already Gone Through the Printer* [*Un enfant de quatre ans est achevé d'imprimer*], Notre-Dame de la Trinité, 1968.

DI: Fr. Gabriel of St. Mary Magdalen, O.C.D., *Divine Intimacy*, TAN, 1996. [Translations found in the text are directly from the French edition, *Intimité divine*, Monastère des carmélites déchaussées, 1957.]

# Bibliography

Dom Guéranger, O.S.B., *The Liturgical Year: Septuagesima* (vol. 4), and *Time after Pentecost, bk. VI*, (vol. 15), Loreto Publications, 2000.

L: Georges Guitton, *Louis Lenoir*, Spes, 1925.

Bishop Harscouët, *Liturgical Perspectives* [*Horizons liturgiques*], Casterman, 1942.

YW: E.M. Lebeau, *Young Women in the Gospel* [*Les jeunes filles dans l'Évangile*], Desclée de Brouwer, 1926.

PA: Claudio Risé, *The Absent Father* [*Le père absent*], Rémi Perrin, 2005.

Paul Vigneron, *History of the Crises in the Modern French Clergy* [*Histoire des crises du clergé français contemporain*], Téqui, 1976.

**Pastoral Letters**

H.E. André du Bois de la Villerabel, Archbishop of Rouen, pastoral letter, 1926.

H.E. André Fauvel, Bishop of Quimper, pastoral letter, 1949.

H.E. Eugène Julien, Bishop of Arras, pastoral letter, 1918.

H.E. Théophile Louvard, Bishop of Coutances, pastoral letter, 1947.

H.E. Marie-Alexis Maisonobe, Bishop of Belley, pastoral letter, 1941.

H.E. Octave Pasquet, Bishop of Séez, pastoral letter, 1927.

H.E. François Picaud, Bishop of Bayeux, pastoral letter, 1939.

H.E. Pierre Rouard, Bishop of Nantes, pastoral letter, 1905.

**Others**

*The Friend of the Clergy* [*L'ami du clergé*], IX, Imprimerie Maitrier et Courtot, 1989.

*The Friend of Parish Clergy* [*L'ami du clergé paroissial*], VI, Imprimerie Maitrier et Courtot, 1894.

*The Friend of Parish Clergy*, XVI and XVIII, Maison Saint-Pierre, 1904 and 1906.

Thomas À Kempis, *The Imitation of Christ*, Penguin Books, 1952.